LYN

FOOD

Gail Duff

Norfolk Library & Information Service
BOOKS WITHDRAWN FOR SALE

30p

GW00694026

PRISM
PRESS

NORFOLK LIBRARY AND
INFORMATION SERVICE

SUPPLIER	B F S
INVOICE No.	N7021807
ORDER DATE	27 APR 1993
COPY No.	

641.555

FAST FOOD, REAL FOOD

Originally published in 1984 under the title *Real Fast Food* by
PRISM PRESS
2 South Street
Bridport
Dorset DT6 3NQ

This revised edition published in 1993

Distributed in the USA by
AVERY PUBLISHING GROUP
120 Old Broadway
Garden City Park
NY 11040

© Gail Duff 1984, 1993

ISBN 1 85327 081 4

All rights reserved. No part of this publication may be reproduced,
stored in a retrieval system, or transmitted, in any form or by any
means, electronic, mechanical, photocopying, recording or otherwise,
without the prior permission of the publishers.

Typeset by Prism Press, Bridport, Dorset.
Printed by The Guernsey Press Ltd, The Channel Islands.

CONTENTS

CHEF'S SPECIAL SALADS 91

Dressings: Vinaigrette — Mayonnaise — Yoghurt — Tahini. *Salads:* Cucumber Pickle — Watercress & Blue Cheese — Crunchy — Cooked Vegetable & Soured Cream — Chicken, Bean & Sesame — Mixed Bean — Egg, Prawn & Crab — Orange — Cheese Platter — Nutty Platter — Mixed Meat Platter.

RELISH TRAY 109

Tomato, Celery and Red Pepper — Sweet Pepper — Mild Onion & Parsley — Corn & Chilli — Sweet Onion & Lime — Lemon & Honey — Sweet & Sour Cucumber — Plum — Apple & Date — Mustard — Horseradish & Orange — Uncooked Cranberry — Mushroom.

PIE STALL 120

Pastry: Double Crust — Turnover — Easy Shortcrust. *Pies:* Spiced Apple — Blueberry & Banana — Cherry — Pumpkin & Yoghurt — Apricot — Honey & Molasses — Honey & Lemon Meringue — Upside Down Apple Cake. *Turnovers:* Apple & Strawberry — Apple & Date — Dried Fruit & Lemon. *Brownies:* Carob — Raisin.

ICE-CREAM PARLOUR 135

Ice-Creams: Vanilla — Strawberry — Butterscotch Pecan — Pina Colada — Banana Yoghurt — Vanilla Yoghurt — Ambrosia Yoghurt — Carob Milk — Maple Syrup & Peanut. *Sherbets:* Apricot & Yoghurt — Cranberry & Yoghurt. *Sauces. Sundaes & Splits:* Strawberry — Carob — Banana. *Iced Lollies:* Orange & Lemon — Apple & Yoghurt.

DRINKS BAR 149

Citrus Cocktail — Fruit Sunrise — Orange, Lemon & Banana Shake — Grapefruit, Pineapple & Banana Crush — Coconut Cocktail — Pineapple Ice Cream Soda — Strawberry Milk Soda — Blackcurrant Yoghurt Fizz — Pink Fizz — Strawberry Yoghurt Shake — Carob Milk Shake I — Carob Milk Shake II.

INTRODUCTION

The fast food boom is here to stay. Young children, teenagers and adults alike enjoy calling into hamburger restaurants and pizza and kebab houses and eating simple, uncomplicated food quickly and with the minimum of fuss. Fast food is chosen for every occasion: for the quick snack after sports; for a reviving meal after a family shopping trip; and even for a birthday when parties of young friends are taken along as well.

It is great to see the family enjoying themselves, but the responsible health conscious mother might well cringe at the thought of greasy burgers in white buns accompanied by soggy French fries. All too often, fast food has acquired a 'junk food' label and, sadly, it is not as nutritious as one would like.

So what can be done about it? The answer, of course, is 'If you can't beat 'em, join 'em'. Do it yourself and give the family the food they want with the nutritional quality that you want. Fast food is fun food and not fancy food and so your task will be an enjoyable one and not difficult.

Once you start, you will realise that fast food need not necessarily be junk food at all. In fact, it can be quite the opposite. Burgers made from pulses or best quality meats, grilled simply and served with home-made, no-sugar relishes provide light, relatively low calorie meals; and what could be healthier than grilling (broiling) steaks and chops to let all the fat drip away? Buns, pizza bases and pitta breads can all be made with wholewheat flour to provide goodness and fibre. Potatoes can be baked in their jackets, and there is no end to the variety of colourful fresh salads that can be made to accompany the main dishes. Fast food meals, well prepared, have a clean, fresh quality that makes them look great and taste great.

Even fast food sweets can be made from healthy ingredients. Use wholewheat flour for pies and turnovers and flavour brownies with carob. Make ice-creams from cream, yoghurt or soya milk, sweeten them with honey and flavour them with fresh fruits. Frothy drinks can be made with yoghurt, milk and sparkling mineral waters and colourful cocktails with natural juices. In your own kitchen, you can keep up with a fast food restaurant any day.

But will the family enjoy staying at home instead of being given the treat of an afternoon or an evening out? For the ordinary everyday family meal or for a snack, they probably won't mind, as on these occasions they will care more about the food they are given than the occasion. If it is to be a special party, however, the atmosphere matters too, so why not turn your dining room into a fast food restaurant for a day?

Play loud music, if that is what they want. Buy bright coloured throw-away napkins and tablecloths and, if they want their meal served in paper cartons and plastic cups, why not? After all, it will save on the washing up! Give out balloons, coloured pencils, badges and paper hats — anything to make the occasion more authentic.

Adults, too, enjoy the relaxed, easy atmosphere of a fast food restaurant. Instead of the formal dinner party at home, try an informal grill or barbeque. You don't have to go as far as paper plates, but bright, check tablecloths, for example, would be ideal. In this case, serve wine instead of shakes and make the cocktails real.

Fast food is a winner with everyone, and, if you prepare it yourself, you will have the satisfaction of knowing that it is nutritionally sound as well as fun to eat.

All the recipes in this book serve 4 people unless otherwise stated.

SANDWICH COUNTER

Sandwiches can make the perfect fast food meal. Most are easy to prepare; you can add enough ingredients to a good quality bread to make them as well balanced nutritionally as any plate of hot food, and you can use colourful ingredients and garnishes to make them look a treat. You can eat a sandwich anytime, anywhere. It makes a relaxed, informal and fun-to-eat meal.

The bread mentioned in all recipes (apart from open sandwiches and crispbreads) is that made from 100% wholewheat flour. For a change, use a ryebread or one made from granary flour. If you make your own bread you can also try substituting either one quarter barley flour or one quarter fine oatmeal for wholewheat flour.

For the open sandwiches, use the types of chewy Scandinavian breads that are cut into thin, rectangular slices and plastic wrapped. Rye bread is mentioned in the recipes but you can also use pumpernickel or other similar types.

For slimmers, always buy wholegrain crispbreads, either rye or wheat. When you are choosing sandwich fillings you can use some old favourites such as ham or cheese and other, more unusual ones, such as mashed cooked pulses or kipper fillets. If you are combining ingredients as in a double decker sandwich, make sure that both flavours and textures go together well. Think also about colour. A sandwich with two layers of a similar nondescript colour may look boring whereas different colours between the slices make a sandwich that is tempting to eat.

When serving sandwiches, cut them into halves or quarters, either diagonally or straight across, for easy eating. Make them look good on the plate. Put them onto a coloured paper napkin and garnish them with small pieces of salad such as watercress sprigs, quartered tomatoes, sliced radishes, apple rings or orange wedges. This way you will be providing a wide range of nutrients besides an enjoyable meal.

Avocado, Tuna & Curd Cheese Sandwiches

Preparation time: 15 minutes
Waiting time: nil
Cooking time: nil

METRIC/IMPERIAL	AMERICAN
1 ripe avocado	1 ripe avocado
one 200 g/7 oz tin tuna fish	one 7 oz tin tuna fish
100 g/4 oz curd cheese	¼ lb curd cheese
grated rind ½ lemon	grated rind ½ lemon
1 tablespoon lemon juice	1 tablespoon lemon juice
½ cucumber	½ cucumber
8 slices wholewheat bread	8 slices wholewheat bread
black olives and tomatoes for serving	black olives and tomatoes for serving

Peel, stone and mash the avocado. Drain and flake the tuna. Pound the avocado, tuna and cheese together. Mix in the lemon rind and juice and pepper.

Thinly slice the cucumber. Butter each slice of bread on one side. Spread 4 slices with the avocado mixture and lay cucumber slices on top. Cover with the remaining bread slices and cut into halves or quarters for serving.

Serve, if wished, with black olives and tomato wedges.

Stilton, Chive & Watercress Sandwiches

Preparation time: 15 minutes
Waiting time: nil
Cooking time: nil

METRIC/IMPERIAL	AMERICAN
175 g/6 oz blue Stilton cheese, grated	1¼ cups grated blue Stilton cheese
6 tablespoons chopped chives	6 tablespoons chopped chives
2 tablespoons chopped parsley	2 tablespoons chopped parsley
1 teaspoon mustard powder	1 teaspoon mustard powder
2 tablespoons single cream	2 tablespoons light cream
8 slices wholewheat bread	8 slices wholewheat bread
butter	butter
75 g/3 oz watercress	3 oz watercress

Put the Stilton into a bowl. Add the herbs and mustard powder and bind the mixture with the cream.

Butter each slice of bread on one side. Press a quarter of the Stilton mixture onto each of the bread slices. Top with watercress sprigs and then put on the remaining slices. Cut the sandwiches into halves or quarters and garnish with the remaining watercress for serving.

Chicken & Caper Sandwiches

Preparation time: 15 minutes
Waiting time: nil
Cooking time: nil

METRIC/IMPERIAL	AMERICAN
225 g/8 oz cooked chicken	8 oz cooked chicken
1 tablespoon chopped capers	1 tablespoon chopped capers
4 tablespoons mayonnaise	¼ cup mayonnaise
8 slices wholewheat bread	8 slices wholewheat bread
butter	butter
16 cucumber slices, unpeeled	16 cucumber slices, unpeeled

Finely chop the chicken. Mix it with the capers and mayonnaise.
   Butter each slice of bread on one side. Lay 4 slices of cucumber on each of 4 pieces of bread. Divide the chicken mixture between the cucumber-topped bread slices. Top with the remaining bread slices.
   Cut the sandwiches into halves or quarters for serving.

Turkey & Peanut Butter Sandwiches

Preparation time: 15 minutes
Waiting time: nil
Cooking time: nil

METRIC/IMPERIAL	AMERICAN
8 slices wholewheat bread	8 slices wholewheat bread
50 g/2 oz crunchy peanut butter	4 tablespoons crunchy
cayenne pepper	peanut butter
225 g/8 oz cooked turkey, sliced	cayenne pepper
4 tablespoons mango chutney	½ lb cooked turkey, sliced
	4 tablespoons mango chutney

Spread the slices of bread on one side with the peanut butter and sprinkle them with cayenne pepper. Lay turkey slices on top of 4 slices of bread and spread them with mango chutney.
   Top with the remaining slices of bread. Cut the sandwiches into halves or quarters for serving.

Ham & Celery Double Deckers

Preparation time: 20 minutes
Waiting time: nil
Cooking time: nil

METRIC/IMPERIAL	AMERICAN
12 slices wholewheat bread	12 slices wholewheat bread
butter	butter
225 g/8 oz cooked lean ham, in four slices equal in size to the bread slices	½ lb cooked lean ham, in four slices equal in size to the bread slices
made English mustard	made English mustard
3 celery sticks, finely chopped	3 celery sticks, finely chopped
2 tablespoons chopped celery leaves, if available	2 tablespoons chopped celery leaves, if available
50 g/2 oz smoked Cheddar cheese finely grated	⅝ cup finely grated smoked Cheddar cheese
3 tablespoons mayonnaise	3 tablespoons mayonnaise

Butter 8 slices of bread on one side only. Butter the remaining four on both sides.

Cover four of the single buttered sides with a slice of ham. Spread the ham with mustard to taste. Put a double buttered slice on top of each ham slice.

Mix together the celery, celery leaves, cheese and mayonnaise. Divide the mixture between the four sandwiches. Put the remaining single buttered slices on top. Cut each sandwich in half.

Cheese Salad Double Deckers

Preparation time: 25 minutes
Waiting time: nil
Cooking time: nil

METRIC/IMPERIAL	AMERICAN
12 slices wholewheat bread	12 slices wholewheat bread
butter	butter
175 g/6 oz Cheddar cheese, finely grated	⅝ cup Cheddar cheese, finely grated
6 tablespoons mayonnaise	⅜ cup mayonnaise
2 tablespoons chopped parsley	2 tablespoons chopped parsley
100 g/4 oz carrots	¼ lb carrots
1 pickled Hungarian gherkin	1 pickled Hungarian gherkin
2 celery sticks	2 celery sticks
½ green pepper	½ sweet green pepper
½ cucumber	½ cucumber
4 small tomatoes	4 small tomatoes

Butter eight slices of bread on one side only. Butter the remaining slices on both sides. Mix together the cheese, mayonnaise and parsley and divide the mixture into two portions. Finely grate the carrots and finely chop the gherkin. Mix them into one portion of the cheese. Finely chop the celery and pepper. Mix them into the remaining cheese. Thinly slice the cucumber and the tomatoes.

Lay the cucumber slices on the buttered side of the single-buttered bread slices. Top them with the celery mixture. Lay a double-buttered slice on top and spread over the carrot mixture. Top with tomato slices and then the remaining single-buttered bread.

Cut the sandwiches in half before serving.

Two Mayonnaise Double Decker

Preparation time: 20 minutes
Waiting time: nil
Cooking time: nil

METRIC/IMPERIAL	AMERICAN
12 slices wholewheat bread	12 slices wholewheat bread
butter	butter
225 g/8 oz cooked butterbeans	1 cup cooked Lima beans
3 tablespoons mayonnaise	3 tablespoons mayonnaise
8 tablespoons chopped parsley	½ cup chopped parsley
2 teaspoons Dijon mustard	2 teaspoons Dijon mustard
freshly ground black pepper	freshly ground black pepper
2 teaspoons chopped capers	2 teaspoons chopped capers
4 small tomatoes	4 small tomatoes
4 eggs, hard boiled	4 hard cooked eggs
1 box mustard and cress	1 box mustard and cress

Butter eight slices of bread on one side only. Butter the remaining slices on both sides.

Mash the beans and mix in half the mayonnaise, half the parsley, half the mustard and some pepper. Spread this bean mixture over four of the single buttered bread slices. Scatter the capers over the beans. Thinly slice the tomatoes and lay them on top. Cover with the double buttered bread slices.

Mash the eggs and mix them with the remaining mayonnaise, parsley and mustard. Season with pepper. Spread the mixture over the double buttered bread slices and top it with mustard and cress. Cover with the remaining bread slices. Cut the sandwiches into halves or quarters for serving.

Sweet & Sour Double Decker

Preparation time: 20 minutes
Waiting time: nil
Cooking time: nil

METRIC/IMPERIAL	AMERICAN
12 slices wholewheat bread	12 slices wholewheat bread
butter	butter
225 g/8 oz curd or other low fat soft cheese	1 cup curd or other low fat soft cheese
4 teaspoons Worcestershire sauce	4 teaspoons Worcestershire sauce
4 teaspoons tamari, soy or shoyu sauce	4 teaspoons tamari, soy or shoyu sauce
4 teaspoons tomato paste	4 teaspoons tomato paste
4 tablespoons chopped parsley	4 tablespoons chopped parsley
4 back bacon rashers	4 back bacon rashers
4 slices fresh pineapple (or pineapple tinned in natural juice)	4 slices fresh pineapple (or pineapple tinned in natural juice)

Butter eight slices of bread on one side and the remaining four slices on both sides. Cream the cheese in a bowl and beat in the sauces, tomato paste and parsley. Grill the bacon rashers.

Spread four single buttered slices of bread with the cheese mixture. Top with the double buttered slices. Cut each bacon rasher in half crossways and lay the pieces on top. Put a pineapple ring on the bacon and top with the remaining bread slices.

Cut the sandwiches into halves or quarters for serving.

Salami Open Sandwiches

Preparation time: 15 minutes
Waiting time: nil
Cooking time: nil

METRIC/IMPERIAL	AMERICAN
4 slices Danish rye bread	4 slices Danish rye bread
25 g/1 oz unsalted butter, softened	2 tablespoons unsalted butter, softened
1 garlic clove, crushed with a pinch sea salt	1 garlic clove, crushed with a pinch sea salt
freshly ground black pepper	freshly ground black pepper
16 thin slices Hungarian or Italian salami	16 thin slices Hungarian or Italian salami
4 black olives	4 black olives
4 slices tomato	4 slices tomato
4 slices pickled cucumber	4 slices pickled cucumber

Cream the butter and beat in the garlic and pepper. Spread it over the slices of bread on one side only. Lay 4 slices of salami on each slice of bread, overlapping as little as possible. Stone the olives and quarter them lengthways. Put an olive quarter on each salami slice, lying lengthways along the bread.

Put a tomato slice in the centre of each open sandwich and top it with a slice of pickled cucumber.

Kipper Open Sandwiches

Preparation time: 15 minutes
Waiting time: 24 hours
Cooking time: nil

METRIC/IMPERIAL	AMERICAN
75 g/3 oz kipper fillet	3 oz kipper fillet
marinade:	*marinade:*
juice ½ lemon	juice ½ lemon
4 tablespoons olive oil	4 tablespoons olive oil
1 teaspoon Dijon mustard	1 teaspoon Dijon mustard
sandwiches:	*sandwiches:*
25 g/1 oz butter	2 tablespoons butter
1 teaspoon Dijon mustard	1 teaspoon Dijon mustard
4 slices rye bread	4 slices rye bread
4 tablespoons chopped parsley	4 tablespoons chopped parsley
1 box mustard and cress	1 box mustard and cress
2 eggs, hard boiled	2 hard cooked eggs
8 small parsley sprigs	8 small parsley sprigs

Skin the kipper fillets and cut them into thin diagonal strips. Beat together the lemon juice, Dijon mustard and olive oil. Turn the kipper strips in this marinade and leave them for 24 hours.

To make the sandwiches, first beat the butter with the Dijon mustard. Spread the mixture over the slices of rye bread. Press parsley and then cress on top of butter. Drain the kipper strips and put a portion in the centre of each slice of bread. Cut the eggs into thin slices and put a slice of egg on each side of the kipper strips.

Top the egg slices with a tiny sprig of parsley.

From the top:
Chicken & Caper Sandwich p. 6.
Cheese, Salad Double Deckers p. 8.

Opposite page 13
Top to bottom:
Salami Open Sandwiches p. 11.
Kipper Open Sandwiches p. 12.
Sesame Crispbreads p. 16.
Liver Sausage Crispbreads p. 14.

Cheese & Ham Open Sandwiches

Preparation time: 15 minutes
Waiting time: nil
Cooking time: nil

METRIC/IMPERIAL	AMERICAN
25 g/1 oz butter	2 tablespoons butter
freshly ground black pepper	freshly ground black pepper
4 slices rye bread	4 slices rye bread
100 g/4 oz lean cooked ham	¼ lb lean cooked ham
4 thin slices Jarlsberg cheese, each the same size as the slices of bread	4 thin slices Jarlsberg cheese, each the same size as the slices of bread
1 small red skinned dessert apple	1 small red skinned dessert apple
1 celery stick	1 celery stick
4 small parsley sprigs	4 small parsley sprigs

Cream the butter with plenty of black pepper. Spread it over the slices of bread. Finely chop the ham and press it on top of the butter. Lay a slice of cheese on top.

Core the apple and cut it into thin lengthways slices. Cut the celery into matchstick sized pieces. Put a small pile of celery in the centre of the cheese and an apple slice on either side.

Garnish with the parsley sprigs.

Liver Sausage Crispbreads

Preparation time: 15 minutes
Waiting time: nil
Cooking time: nil

METRIC/IMPERIAL	AMERICAN
150 g/5 oz liver sausage	5 oz liver sausage
25 g/1 oz butter	2 tablespoons butter
4 rye crispbreads	4 rye crispbreads
4 spring onions, finely chopped	4 spring onions, finely chopped
4 stuffed olives	4 stuffed olives
4 radish slices	4 radish slices

In a bowl, cream together 25 g/1 oz of the liver sausage and the butter. Spread this mixture over the crispbreads. Press the chopped spring onions on top. Cut the remaining liver sausage into four slices. Put a slice into the centre of each crispbread.

Cut each olive into 4 slices. Put a radish slice in the centre of the liver sausage and arrange the olive slices round it.

Prawn Crispbreads

Preparation time: 20 minutes
Waiting time: nil
Cooking time: nil

METRIC/IMPERIAL	AMERICAN
100 g/4 oz shelled prawns	⅝ cup shelled shrimp
25 g/1 oz butter or low fat spread	2 tablspoons butter or low fat spread
2 teaspoons tomato paste	2 teaspoons tomato paste
pinch cayenne pepper	pinch cayenne pepper
grated rind 1 lemon	grated rind 1 lemon
4 crispbreads	4 crispbreads
50 g/2 oz curd cheese	2 oz curd cheese
2 tablespoons soured cream	2 tablspoons soured cream
16 slices cucumber	16 slices cucumber
paprika	paprika
20 capers	20 capers

Cream the butter and beat in the tomato paste, cayenne pepper and lemon rind. Spread the butter over the crispbreads.

Beat the curd cheese to a cream and beat in the soured cream. Fold in the prawns. Put a portion of prawns in the centre of each crispbread. Put 2 cucumber rings on either side. Sprinkle a very little paprika over the prawns.

Put a whole caper on top of the prawns and on each of the cucumber slices.

Sesame Crispbreads

Preparation time: 15 minutes
Waiting time: nil
Cooking time: nil

METRIC/IMPERIAL	AMERICAN
2 tablespoons tahini (sesame paste)	2 tablespoons tahini (sesame paste)
2 tablespoons tamari, shoyu or soy sauce	2 tablespoons tamari, shoyu or soy sauce
2 teaspoons tomato paste	2 teaspoons tomato paste
grated rind and juice ½ medium orange	grated rind and juice ½ medium orange
½ garlic clove, crushed	½ garlic clove, crushed
4 rye crispbreads	4 rye crispbreads
1 teaspoon sesame seeds	1 teaspoon sesame seeds
1 red pepper	1 sweet red pepper
2 tomatoes	2 tomatoes
4 black olives	4 black olives

Mix together the tahini, tamari, tomato paste, orange rind and juice and garlic. Spread the mixture over the crispbreads and sprinkle sesame seeds over the top.

Core, seed and finely chop the pepper. Scatter the pieces over the sesame seeds. Cut each tomato into four slices and put two on each crispbread. Halve and stone the olives. Put half on each tomato slice.

Although these look very light, they are in fact extremely filling.

BURGER HOUSE

Burgers, particularly those made from beef, have come to symbolise fast food more than any other type of meal. They can be cooked in minutes and, when put into a bun, are as easy to eat as sandwiches. A bought burger made from over-fat meat and put into a white flour bun is not particularly nutritious. A home made one, containing only lean meat or even cunningly made without meat at all, and put into a wholewheat bun with a garnish of salad is quite a different story. Home made burgers also always taste better than the bought kinds.

Meat Burgers

If you can buy a good quality, very lean, ready minced (ground) meat, then do so. If not mince (grind) it yourself. For beef burgers, choose any good quality braising steak such as chuck. Lamb burgers are best made from the shoulder or leg; and you can make pork burgers from the spare rib, hand and spring and the lean end of the belly.

Chicken burgers can be made from either breast or leg meat or a mixture. Buy ready boned meat or bone it yourself. One 1.35 kg/3 lb chicken will give about 450 g/1 lb meat. Buy boned turkey meat for burgers.

Whichever type of meat that you choose, make sure that you remove most of the fat. Allow 100 g/4 oz minced (ground) meat per burger. One should be enough for each person with a bun, a salad and perhaps a baked potato.

If you have a food processor, meat for burgers can be prepared most successfully in that. It can also be put through a rotary mincer (grinder). For plain burgers you need only season them well with freshly ground black pepper. After this, you can make the mixtures as complicated as you like. Add a little spice such as paprika, or various mixtures of chopped fresh herbs and small amounts of dried herbs. Grated raw onion or crushed garlic will also add to the flavour.

It is possible to form well shaped, flat burgers by hand, but if you make them often it would be well worth your while buying a small plastic burger press. This ensures that they will all be of an even size and shape and burgers made in a press tend to hold together better than the hand made ones.

Press the burgers out onto a flat plate or chopping board and then put them into the refrigerator for 30 minutes at least to chill and set into shape.

You can cook burgers under a conventional grill (broiler), on a ridged, cast iron grill (broiler) on top of the stove or on a barbeque. If you are using the conventional oven, check to make sure that the grill rack is suitable. If it consists only of a thin wire grid, then cover it with aluminium foil into which you have punched one or two fine holes through which the fat can get away. Heat the grill (broiler) with the rack and foil in place for at least 4 minutes before cooking the burgers.

If using a cast iron grill (broiler) oil it lightly first and then heat it on a high heat until it begins to smoke. Lower the heat before starting to cook. This prevents burning while maintaining a high temperature.

When cooking burgers over a barbeque, use a special holder which usually holds four burgers at once. It is made from a closer mesh than the barbeque grid and so will prevent the burgers from breaking up and falling into the coals. Cook the burgers over coals that are glowing red.

COOKING TIME FOR MEAT BURGERS (MINUTES EACH SIDE)

	Rare	Medium	Well Done
Beef	1½ minutes	2½ minutes	3½ minutes
Lamb	not recommended	2½ minutes	3½–4 minutes
Pork	not recommended	not recommended	3½–4 minutes
Chicken	not recommended	not recommended	4 minutes
Turkey	not recommended	not recommended	4 minutes

Vegetarian Burgers

Vegetarian burgers are every bit as tasty as meat ones and the variety of flavours that you can achieve is surprising. All types of lentils make superb burgers. When using beans, choose those with stronger flavours and darker colours such as red, brown and black kidney beans, aduki beans, mung beans and field and pinto beans.

Cook all pulses for burgers until they are tender but not falling apart. Drain them well, cool them completely and then mash them. You will achieve a better texture with a heavy potato masher than with a liquidiser or food processor.

Sharper flavours such as tomato, lemon and vinegar all help to lighten the flavour of vegetarian burgers. Vegetables can be added for interest in texture and cereals such as millet or burghul wheat can be included in the mixture when whole lentils are used to help in holding the burgers together.

When forming the burgers, again use a burger press. It is best to coat them in flour for cooking. The best way to do this is to thickly coat a flat plate or chopping board with wholewheat flour and press the burgers out onto it. Then sprinkle them with more flour. Chill vegetarian burgers for at least 45 minutes before cooking, the longer the better.

Cook bean burgers under a conventional grill or on a broiler so that they brown on both sides.

Serving Meat and Vegetarian Burgers

Some of the burger recipes below have their own toppings or sauces, others can be served plainly and accompanied by several of the relishes on pages 109-119. Finely chopped raw onion and a mild American mustard will also help you to achieve an authentic fast food atmosphere and flavour.

Always use wholewheat buns or baps. These are becoming easier to find in most bakers' shops and supermarkets. If you are serving an eat-in-the-hand complete meal, top the burger with small pieces of salad. If you are serving it on a plate then make the salad larger. Some like to have a burger, a bun and a baked potato.

If you have a smaller appetite serve either bun or potato.

Herby Burgers

Preparation time: 20 minutes
Waiting time: 30 minutes
Cooking time: 3-7 minutes

METRIC/IMPERIAL	AMERICAN
450 g/1 lb minced beef	1 lb ground beef
1 small onion	1 small onion
2 teaspoons dried mixed herbs	2 teaspoons dried mixed herbs
sea salt and freshly ground black pepper	sea salt and freshly ground black pepper

Put the beef into a bowl. Grate in the onion and add the herbs and seasonings. Mix well.

Form the mixture into four burger shapes and chill for 30 minutes before grilling.

Parsley Burgers

Preparation time: 20 minutes
Waiting time: 30 minutes
Cooking time: 3-7 minutes

METRIC/IMPERIAL	AMERICAN
450 g/1 lb minced beef	1 lb ground beef
6 tablespoons chopped parsley	⅜ cup chopped parsley
1 garlic clove with a pinch of sea salt	1 garlic clove crushed with a pinch of sea salt
3 tablespoons Worcestershire sauce	3 tablespoons Worcestershire sauce

Put the beef into a bowl. Add the parsley, garlic and Worcestershire sauce. Mix well, making sure that the garlic becomes well distributed.

Form the mixture into four burger shapes and chill them for 30 minutes before grilling.

Suggested relishes: Tomato and red pepper; Mushroom; Sweet onion and Lime.

Spice Burgers

Preparation time: 20 minutes
Waiting time: 30 minutes
Cooking time: 3-7 minutes

METRIC/IMPERIAL	AMERICAN
450 g/1 lb minced beef	1 lb ground beef
½ teaspoon black peppercorns	½ teaspoon black peppercorns
4 juniper berries	4 juniper berries
4 allspice berries	4 allspice berries
pinch sea salt	pinch sea salt
1 garlic clove, finely chopped	1 garlic clove, finely chopped
2 sage leaves, finely chopped	2 sage leaves, finely chopped

Put the beef into a bowl. Using a pestle and mortar, crush together the peppercorns, juniper and allspice berries, salt and garlic. Add these and the sage to the beef and mix well to make sure they become well incorporated.

Form the mixture into four burger shapes. Leave them in a cool place for 30 minutes before grilling.

Curry Burgers with Hot Lentil Sauce

BURGERS:	SAUCE:
Preparation time: 20 minutes	Preparation time: 15 minutes
Waiting time: 30 minutes	Waiting time: nil
Cooking time 3-7 minutes	Cooking time: nil

METRIC/IMPERIAL	AMERICAN
burgers:	*burgers:*
450 g/1 lb minced beef	1 lb ground beef
1 small onion, grated	1 small onion, grated
2 tablespoons tomato paste	2 tablespoons tomato paste
2 teaspoons hot curry powder	2 teaspoons hot curry powder
½ teaspoon ground cumin	½ teaspoon ground cumin
½ teaspoon ground coriander	½ teaspoon ground coriander
¼ teaspoon ground ginger	¼ teaspoon ground ginger
sauce:	*sauce:*
2 tablespoons sunflower oil	2 tablespoons sunflower oil
1 medium onion, finely chopped	1 medium onion, finely chopped
1 garlic clove, finely chopped	1 garlic clove, finely chopped
50 g/2 oz split red lentils	¼ cup split red lentils
½ teaspoon ground cumin	½ teaspoon ground cumin
½ teaspoon ground coriander	½ teaspoon ground coriander
¼ teaspoon chilli powder	¼ teaspoon chilli powder
pinch ground ginger	pinch ground ginger
one 400 g/14 oz tin tomatoes in tomato juice	one 14 oz tin tomatoes in tomato juice
1 bayleaf	1 bayleaf

Put the beef into a bowl and thoroughly mix in the onion, tomato paste and spices. Make the mixture into 8 round burgers and put them into the refrigerator for 30 minutes to set into shape.

For the sauce, heat the oil in a saucepan on a low heat. Mix in the onion and garlic and soften them. Stir in the lentils and spices and cook stirring, for 2 minutes. Pour in the tomatoes and their juice. Bring to the boil and add the bayleaf.

Cover and simmer for 45 minutes so the lentils have softened and mixed with the tomatoes to make a thick sauce.

Yoghurt Beef Burgers with Onions

Preparation time: 40 minutes
Waiting time: 30 minutes
Cooking time: 3-7 minutes

METRIC/IMPERIAL	AMERICAN
450 g/1 lb minced beef	1 lb ground beef
3 tablespoons chopped mint	3 tablespoons chopped mint
6 sage leaves, chopped	6 sage leaves, chopped
grated rind 1 lemon	grated rind 1 lemon
4 tablespoons olive or sunflower oil	¼ cup olive or sunflower oil
1 medium onion, finely chopped	1 medium onion, finely chopped
1 garlic clove, finely chopped	1 garlic clove, finely chopped
topping:	*topping:*
3 tablespoons olive or sunflower oil	3 tablespoons olive or sunflower oil
2 large onions, quartered and thinly sliced	2 large onions, quartered and thinly sliced
juice 1 lemon	juice 1 lemon
1 tablespoon natural yoghurt	1 tablespoon natural yoghurt
2 tablespoons chopped mint	2 tablespoons chopped mint

Put the beef into a mixing bowl and beat in the mint, sage and lemon rind. Heat the oil in a frying pan on a low heat, mix in the onion and garlic and cook them until they are just beginning to soften. Beat them into the beef and form the mixture into four burger shapes. Put them into the refrigerator for 30 minutes to set into shape.

For the topping: heat the oil in a frying pan on a low heat. Mix in the onions and soften them.

Pour in the lemon juice and let it bubble and reduce by half. Take the pan from the heat and let the onions cool a little. Mix in the yoghurt and mint.

Grill the burgers. They can either be served hot with a hot topping; or, for a salad meal, let them both cool completely.

Chilli Bean Burgers

BURGERS:
Preparation time: 25 minutes
Waiting time: 30 minutes
Cooking time: 4-7 minutes

BEAN TOPPING:
Preparation time: 15 minutes
Waiting time: nil
Cooking time: 15 minutes

METRIC/IMPERIAL	AMERICAN
225 g/8 oz red kidney beans, soaked and cooked	1¼ cups red kidney beans, soaked and cooked
225 g/8 oz minced beef	½ lb ground beef
1 small onion	1 small onion
2 red chillies	2 red chillies
2 tablespoons tomato paste	2 tablespoons tomato paste
350 g/12 oz tomatoes	¾ lb tomatoes
4 tablespoons oil	¼ cup oil
1 large onion, thinly sliced	1 large onion, thinly sliced
1 garlic clove, finely chopped	1 garlic clove, finely chopped

Mash or purée half the cooked beans. Beat them with the beef. Grate in the onion. Core, seed and finely chop the chillies and add half of one of them to the bean mixture. Beat in the tomato purée. Form the mixture into four flat burgers and chill them for 30 minutes.

Scald and skin the tomatoes. Heat 2 tablespoons of the oil in a saucepan on a low heat. Put in the onion and garlic and soften them. Mix in the tomatoes and beans. Cover and simmer them gently for 15 minutes.

Oil the griddle well and cook the burgers until they are browned on each side and cooked through. Serve them topped with the simmered beans and tomatoes.

Lamb & Green Pepper Burgers

BURGERS:	TOPPING:
Preparation time: 20 minutes	*Preparation time: 10 minutes*
Waiting time: 30 minutes	*Waiting time: nil*
Cooking time: 5-8 minutes	*Cooking time: 10 minutes*

METRIC/IMPERIAL	AMERICAN
450 g/1 lb minced lamb	1 lb ground lamb
1 green pepper	1 sweet green pepper
1 red pepper	1 sweet red pepper
1 garlic clove crushed with a pinch sea salt	1 garlic clove crushed with a pinch sea salt
2 tablespoons tomato paste	2 tablespoons tomato paste
2 teaspoons ground coriander	2 teaspoons ground coriander
freshly ground black pepper	freshly ground black pepper
1 small aubergine	1 small egg-plant
225 g/8 oz tomatoes	½ lb tomatoes
4 tablespoons oil	4 tablespoons oil
1 medium onion, finely chopped	1 medium onion, finely chopped
1 garlic clove, finely chopped	1 garlic clove, finely chopped

Put the lamb into a bowl. Core, seed and finely dice the peppers. Mix half the green pepper into the lamb. Add the crushed garlic, the tomato paste and half the coriander. Season with the black pepper. Form the mixture into four burgers. Put them onto a flat plate or a board and chill them for 30 minutes.

Finely dice the aubergine. Scald, skin and finely dice the tomatoes. Heat the oil in a saucepan on a low heat. Add the onion and chopped garlic and soften them. Mix in the remaining coriander, the peppers and aubergine. Cover and cook gently for 5 minutes. Mix in the tomatoes. Cover and cook for a further 5 minutes.

Grill the burgers for 5 minutes each side or until they are browned and cooked through. Serve them topped with the pepper and aubergine mixture.

Lamb, Herb & Cheese Burgers

Preparation time: 20 minutes
Waiting time: 30 minutes
Cooking time: 5-8 minutes

METRIC/IMPERIAL	AMERICAN
450 g/1 lb minced lamb	1 lb ground lamb
1 garlic clove, crushed with pinch sea salt	1 garlic clove, crushed with pinch sea salt
3 tablespoons chopped parsley	3 tablespoons chopped parsley
1 tablespoon chopped thyme	1 tablespoon chopped thyme
1 tablespoon chopped marjoram	1 tablespoon chopped marjoram
2 teaspoons chopped rosemary	2 teaspoons chopped rosemary
freshly ground black pepper	freshly ground black pepper
100 g/4 oz Gruyère cheese cut into four 5 cm/2" square slices	¼ lb Gruyère cheese cut into 2" square slices
100 g/4 oz Gruyère cheese, grated (optional)	1 cup grated Gruyère cheese (optional)

Put the lamb into a bowl and beat in the garlic, herbs and pepper. Divide the mixture into four.

Put half of one of the portions into a burger press in an even layer. Press a square of cheese on top and then put in the remaining lamb. Form the rest in the same way. Put the burgers onto a flat plate or board and chill them for 30 minutes.

Grill the burgers. Just before serving, scatter the remaining cheese over the top.

Pork & Apple Burgers

Preparation time: 20 minutes
Waiting time: 30 minutes
Cooking time: 7-8 minutes

METRIC/IMPERIAL	AMERICAN
450 g/1 lb minced pork	1 lb ground pork
1 large cooking apple	1 large cooking apple
1 small onion	1 small onion
½ teaspoon black peppercorns	½ teaspoon black peppercorns
pinch sea salt	pinch sea salt
1 garlic clove, finely chopped	1 garlic clove, finely chopped

Put the pork into a bowl. Peel and core the apple and grate it into the pork. Grate in the onion. Using a pestle and mortar, crush together the peppercorns, salt and garlic. Add them to the pork and mix well. Form the mixture into four flat burgers and refrigerate them for 30 minutes before grilling (broiling).
Suggested relish: Mustard.

Pork & Bacon Burgers

Preparation time: 20 minutes
Waiting time: 30 minutes
Cooking time: 7-8 minutes

METRIC/IMPERIAL	AMERICAN
450 g/1 lb minced pork	1 lb ground pork
2 rashers lean back bacon, finely chopped	2 rashers lean back bacon, finely chopped
2 teaspoons spiced granular mustard	2 teaspoons spiced granular mustard
1 small onion, grated	1 small onion, grated
3 sage leaves, chopped	4 sage leaves, chopped

Mix all the ingredients together and beat them with a wooden spoon to incorporate them well. Form the mixture into four flat burgers and refrigerate them for 30 minutes before grilling (broiling).

Chicken Burgers with Spiced Onions

Preparation time: 25 minutes
Waiting time: 30 minutes
Cooking time: 8 minutes

METRIC/IMPERIAL	AMERICAN
450 g/1 lb boned chicken meat	1 lb boned chicken meat
25 g/1 oz parsley, finely chopped	½ cup chopped parsley
grated rind and juice 1 lemon	grated rind and juice 1 lemon
freshly ground black pepper	freshly ground black pepper
25 g/1 oz butter	2 tablespoons butter
2 medium onions, finely chopped	2 medium onions, finely chopped
1 teaspoon ground cumin	1 teaspoon ground cumin

Finely mince (grind) the chicken. Add the parsley, lemon rind and pepper and mix well. Form the mixture into four burgers and chill them for 30 minutes.

Just before cooking, prepare the onions. Melt the butter in a frying pan on a very low heat. Stir in the onions and cumin and cook until the onions are soft but not coloured. Pour in the lemon juice and let it boil. Keep the onions warm.

Grill (broil) the burgers as above and top them with the spiced onions.

Clockwise from top left:
Black-eyed beans & Tomato Burgers p. 30.
Curry Burgers with Hot Lentil Sauce p. 22.
Chicken Burgers with Spiced Onions p. 28.
Lamb & Green Pepper Burgers p. 25.

Opposite page 29:
Top to bottom:
Nutty Lentil Burgers p. 29.
Aduki Burgers with Onion Topping p. 31.
Turkey & Cranberry Burgers p. 33.

Nutty Lentil Burgers

BURGERS:
Preparation time: 1¼ hours
Waiting time: 45 minutes
Cooking time: 4 minutes

TOPPING:
Preparation time: 10 minutes
Waiting time: nil
Cooking time: 15 minutes

METRIC/IMPERIAL	AMERICAN
225 g/8 oz red lentils	1 cup red lentils
1 large onion, finely chopped	1 large onion, finely chopped
1 garlic clove, crushed	1 garlic clove, crushed
450 ml/¾ pint cold water	2 cups cold water
1 bayleaf	1 bayleaf
freshly ground black pepper	freshly ground black pepper
75 g/3 oz walnuts	¾ cup walnut meats
2 tablespoons tomato paste	2 tablespoons tomato paste
2 tablespoons tamari, shoyu or soy sauce	2 tablespoons tamari, shoyu or soy sauce
2 teaspoons dried mixed herbs	2 teaspoons dried mixed herbs
topping:	*topping:*
350 g/12 oz tomatoes	¾ lb tomatoes
1 red pepper	1 sweet red pepper
100 g/4 oz mushrooms	¼ lb mushrooms
1 small onion	1 small onion
2 tablespoons oil	2 tablespoons oil
1 garlic clove, finely chopped	1 garlic clove, finely chopped
2 tablespoons tamari, shoyu or soy sauce	2 tablespoons tamari, shoyu or soy sauce

Put the lentils, onion, garlic, water and bayleaf into a saucepan. Season with the pepper. Bring them gently to the boil, cover tightly and cook on a very low heat, stirring once or twice, until all the water has been absorbed and the lentils are reduced to a soft purée. Take them from the heat and cool them completely. Remove the bayleaf.

Finely grind the walnuts and mix them into the lentils together with the tomato paste, tamari sauce and herbs. Form the mixture into eight burgers. Coat them in flour and chill them for 45 minutes.

For the topping, scald, skin and chop the tomatoes. Core, seed and finely chop the pepper. Finely chop the mushrooms and onion. Heat the oil in a frying pan on a low heat. Put in the pepper, mushrooms, onion and garlic, cover and cook for 5 minutes or until they begin to soften. Put in the tomatoes and tamari sauce, cover again and cook for 10 minutes.

Grill the burgers as directed and serve topped with the hot sauce.

Black-Eyed Bean & Tomato Burgers

BEANS:	BURGERS:
Preparation time: 2¼ hours	Preparation time: 15 minutes
(including soaking)	Waiting time: 45 minutes
Cooking time: 45 minutes	Cooking time: 4 minutes

METRIC/IMPERIAL	AMERICAN
225 g/8 oz black-eyed beans	1 cup black-eyed beans
2 tablespoons oil	2 tablespoons oil
1 large onion, finely chopped	1 large onion, finely chopped
1 garlic clove, finely chopped	1 garlic clove, finely chopped
575 ml/1 pint stock	2½ cups stock
3 tablespoons tomato paste	3 tablespoons tomato paste
1 teaspoon paprika	1 teaspoon paprika
2 teaspoons dried mixed herbs	2 teaspoon dried mixed herbs
25 g/1 oz wholewheat flour	¼ cup wholewheat flour
4 tomatoes	4 tomatoes
100 g/4 oz Gruyère cheese, grated	1 cup grated Gruyère cheese

Put the beans into a saucepan and cover them with water. Bring them to the boil, boil them for 5 minutes and take the pan from the heat. Leave the beans for 2 hours. Drain them.

Heat the oil in a saucepan on a low heat. Put in the onion and garlic and soften them. Pour in the stock and bring it to the boil. Add the beans, tomato paste, paprika and herbs. Cover and simmer for 45 minutes or until the beans are tender. If there is still some liquid left, uncover the pan, raise the heat and stir until it has evaporated.

Cool the beans completely. Mash them. Form them into 8 round burger shapes, coat them in the flour and chill them for 45 minutes.

Heat an oiled grill (broiler) on a high heat. When it is hot, turn down the heat. Grill (broil) the burgers until they are brown on each side.

To serve, top them with grated cheese. Cut each tomato into four slices and put two slices on the top of each burger.

Aduki Burgers with Onion Topping

BEANS:	BURGERS:
Preparation time: 12 hours	Preparation time: 30 minutes
(including soaking)	Waiting time: 45 minutes
Cooking time: 45 minutes	Cooking time 4 minutes

Preparation time for topping: 15 minutes

METRIC/IMPERIAL	AMERICAN
225 g/8 oz aduki beans	1 cup aduki beans
1 green pepper	1 sweet green pepper
2 celery sticks	2 celery sticks
1 large onion	1 large onion
1 garlic clove	1 garlic clove
3 tablespoons oil	3 tablespoons oil
2 teaspoons miso (soya paste)	2 teaspoons miso (soya paste)
3 tablespoons cold water	3 tablespoons cold water
2 teaspoons dried mixed herbs	2 teaspoons dried mixed herbs
topping:	*topping:*
4 tablespoons oil	¼ cup oil
2 large onions, finely chopped	2 large onions, finely chopped
2 teaspoons dried mixed herbs	2 teaspoons dried mixed herbs
1 tablespoon miso (soya paste)	1 tablespoon miso (soya paste)
6 tablespoons white wine vinegar	⅜ cup white wine vinegar

Soak the aduki beans overnight and cook them for 45 minutes or until tender. Drain, cool and mash them. Core, seed and finely chop the pepper. Finely chop the celery, onion and garlic. Heat the oil in a frying pan on a low heat. Mix in the pepper, celery, onion and garlic and cook them gently, stirring frequently, until the onion browns. Mix the miso with the water to make a smooth paste. Mix the vegetables, miso paste and herbs into the mashed beans. Form the mixture into eight burgers and chill them for at least 45 minutes.

For the topping, heat the oil in a frying pan on a low heat. Put in the onions and herbs and cook until the onions are soft. Mix the miso with the vinegar to make a smooth paste. Pour it into the pan and bring it to the boil. Serve the grilled burgers with the hot topping spooned over them.

Brown Lentil Burgers with Barbeque Sauce

BURGERS:	TOPPING:
Preparation time: 1½ hours	Preparation time: 15 minutes
Waiting time: 45 minutes	Waiting time: nil
Cooking time: 4 minutes	Cooking time: 30-40 minutes

METRIC/IMPERIAL	AMERICAN
225 g/8 oz brown lentils	1¼ cups brown lentils
50 g/2 oz millet	¼ cup millet
1 large onion finely chopped	1 large onion finely chopped
1 garlic clove finely chopped	1 garlic clove finely chopped
1 bayleaf	1 bayleaf
2 tablespoons Worcestershire sauce	2 tablespoons Worcestershire sauce
2 tablespoons tamari, shoyu or soy sauce	2 tablespoons tamari, shoyu or soy sauce
1 tablespoon tomato paste	1 tablespoon tomato paste
sauce:	*sauce:*
4 tablespoons oil	¼ cup oil
2 large onions, finely chopped	2 large onions, finely chopped
2 garlic cloves, finely chopped	2 garlic cloves, finely chopped
450 g/1 lb tomatoes, scalded, skinned and chopped	1 lb tomatoes, scalded, skinned and chopped
4 tablespoons Worcestershire sauce	¼ cup Worcestershire sauce
4 tablespoons tamari, shoyu or soy sauce	¼ cup tamari, shoyu or soy sauce
2 tablespoons white wine vinegar	2 tablespoons white wine vinegar
2 tablespoons dark barbados sugar	2 tablespoons dark barbados sugar

To make the burgers, put the lentils, millet, onion and garlic into a saucepan with 575 ml/1 pint/2½ cups water and the bayleaf. Bring them to the boil, cover and simmer for 45 minutes or until both lentils and millet are tender and the water has been completely absorbed. Remove the bayleaf. Mash and cool them completely.

Beat in the Worcestershire sauce, tamari sauce and tomato paste. Form the mixture into eight burgers. Chill them for at least 45 minutes.

To make the sauce, heat the oil in a frying pan on a low heat. Put in the onion and garlic and cook until the onion is transparent. Stir in the remaining ingredients. Bring them to the boil. Simmer, uncovered, until the sauce is thick, 30-40 minutes.

Cook the burgers as directed and serve topped with the hot sauce.

Turkey & Cranberry Burgers

Preparation time: 30 minutes
Waiting time: 30 minutes
Cooking time: 8 minutes

METRIC/IMPERIAL	AMERICAN
450 g/1 lb boned turkey meat	1 lb boned turkey meat
50 g/2 oz cooked lean ham	2 oz cooked lean ham
50 g/2 oz cranberries	¼ cup cranberries
25 g/1 oz butter	2 tablespoons butter
1 small onion, finely chopped	1 small onion, finely chopped
2 tablespoons chopped parsley	2 tablespoons chopped parsley
1 tablespoon chopped thyme	1 tablespoon chopped thyme
4 sage leaves, chopped	4 sage leaves, chopped
freshly ground black pepper	freshly ground black pepper

Finely mince (grind) together the turkey and ham. Finely chop the cranberries.

Melt the butter in a frying pan on a low heat. Put in the cranberries and onion and cook until the onion is soft. Add them to the turkey and ham. Add the herbs and pepper and mix well.

Form the mixture into four burgers. Chill them for 30 minutes and grill them as above.

Serve with Cranberry Relish.

BARBEQUE GRILL

Grilled (broiled) meats can be prepared for any occasion. They take up very little time and can be cooked in minutes. This makes them ideal for week-day family meals when people's coming home times are not certain. Yet because most grills are produced from the better quality meats, they are suitable for serving at dinner parties, especially when you have used an unusual marinade or topping.

Meat that has been cooked skilfully in this manner retains all its flavour and loses a certain amount of its undesirable fat. This, combined with the fact that no heavy sauces are involved in the preparation, makes a grill a healthy meal.

One thing to always remember is that grilled meats are spoiled if they have to be kept hot. You must therefore have the meat all ready to go before you start the first course and then not be afraid to cook between courses.

Cuts for grilling

Grilling is a quick process and so you need to buy tender cuts of meat. Fillet of beef, cut into 2.5–4 cm/1–1½ inch thick slices is the most expensive, but many people prefer the flavour and size of slices cut from the rump or sirloin, again about 2.5 cm/1 inch thick. An entrecôte steak is a slice taken from the top of the sirloin. A T-bone, cut 4–5 cm/1½–2 inches thick, is a whole slice from the sirloin. A porterhouse steak, usually 4–5 cm/1½–2 inches thick, is a slice from the wing rib taken from the bone. All these are suitable for the following recipes, apart from the Beef Teriyaki for which fillet must be used. 175 g/6 oz per person should be ample but larger steaks may be used provided that the width and not the thickness of the meat is increased.

If you are cooking lamb, choose loin chops or cutlets taken from the best end neck. Noisettes, made by boning and rolling the best end neck before cutting are also suitable. Lamb chops are usually on the small side so cook two per person. If they are large, one plus a topping should be sufficient.

Pork chops are cut usually about 2 cm/¾ inch thick from either the loin or the spare rib. Pork ribs, provided they have been marinated first, can also be grilled. For these, always use a grill on a conventional cooker or a barbeque over coals. They are not sufficiently flat to cook evenly on a cast iron grill (broiler).

Preparation

Before grilling, brush all meats with a little oil and season lightly with pepper only. Salt causes valuable juices to escape. No matter how tender the cut of meat, it will always be improved by marinating for 4 hours or even longer.

Cooking

All the mentioned cuts of meat, apart from the pork ribs, can be cooked on a conventional grill, on a cast iron grill (broiler) or over barbeque coals.

When using a conventional grill, preheat it for 5–6 minutes before cooking with the grill pan and cooking rack in place. If the meat looks as though it is cooking too quickly, lower the rack rather than the temperature.

Always lightly oil a cast iron grill (broiler) and heat it on a high temperature until it begins to smoke. Put the meat on it and immediately lower the heat.

When cooking meat over barbeque coals start it off on aluminium foil to prevent any fat from raising the flames and burning the meat. Prick the foil in several places with a fine skewer to let the fat escape. Heat it on the barbeque grid for 5 minutes, put on the meat and sear both sides. When most of the fat has dripped away, carefully remove the foil and finish cooking the meat over the glowing (not flaming) coals.

Serving grills

Grilled meats are best if they are served plainly with well chosen relishes if required and accompanied by a salad and a baked potato.

COOKING TIMES (MINUTES EACH SIDE)

	Rare	Medium	Well Done
Beef			
Rump	3–3½	4–5	7–8
2.5 cm/1 inch thick			
Sirloin or entrecôte	2½	3–3½	4½–5
2.5 cm/1 inch thick			
T-Bone	3½–4	4–5	5½–7
4–5 cm/1½–2 inches thick			
Porterhouse	3½–4	4–5	5½–7
4–5 cm/1½–2 inches thick			
Lamb			
Best end neck cutlets or noisettes	*	3½–4	4½–5
2–2.5 cm/¾–1 inch thick			
Loin chops	*	4–5	5½–7
2.5–5 cm 1–1½ inches thick			
Pork			
Loin chops	*	*	5½–7
2 cm/¾ inches thick			
Spare rib chops	*	*	5½–7
2 cm/¾ inches thick			
Pork ribs			

— for well done cook for a total of 20 minutes, turning frequently.

* not recommended

Steak Marinated with Wine & Lemon

Preparation time: 15 minutes
Waiting time: 4-6 hours
Cooking time: 5-10 minutes

METRIC/IMPERIAL	AMERICAN
675 g/1½ lbs rump or sirloin steak	1½ lbs rump or sirloin steak
50 g/2 oz butter	4 tablespoons butter
6 tablespoons dry red wine	⅜ cup dry red wine
grated rind and juice 1 lemon	grated rind and juice 1 lemon
2 tablespoons chopped thyme	2 tablespoons chopped thyme
2 tablespoons chopped marjoram	2 tablespoons chopped marjoram
sea salt and freshly ground black pepper	sea salt and freshly ground black pepper

Cut the steak into 4 even sized pieces. Put the butter into a small saucepan and melt it on a low heat without letting it bubble. Remove it from the heat and add the wine and lemon juice. Pour the mixture into a large flat dish, big enough to take the steak in a single layer and mix in the lemon rind and herbs.

Turn the steak in the marinade and season it well on both sides. Cover it and leave it for 4-6 hours at room temperature.

Grill to your liking.

Steak with Orange

Preparation time: 15 minutes
Waiting time: 4 hours
Cooking time: 5-10 minutes

METRIC/IMPERIAL	AMERICAN
675–900 g/1½–2 lb rump or sirloin steak	1½–2 lb rump or sirloin steak
marinade:	*marinade:*
juice 1 large orange	juice 1 large orange
4 tablespoons olive oil	4 tablespoons olive oil
¼ teaspoon celery salt	¼ teaspoon celery salt
1 tablespoon chopped thyme	1 tablespoon chopped thyme
1 garlic clove, crushed	1 garlic clove, crushed
garnish:	*garnish:*
2 large oranges	2 large oranges
75 g/3 oz watercress	3 oz watercress

Cut the steak into four even sized pieces. Mix together the marinade ingredients and put them into a flat dish. Turn the steak in the marinade and leave it for 4 hours at room temperature, turning several times.

Cut the rind and pith from the remaining oranges and thinly slice the flesh. Lift the steak from the marinade and grill (broil) it to your liking. If using a conventional grill (broiler) lay orange slices over the steak about 1 minute before it is done to let them heat through. If using a cast iron grill (broiler), remove the steak and keep it warm. Lay the orange slices on the grill (broiler) and cook them for about a minute so they heat through. Lay them on the steak to serve.

Garnish with watercress.

Grilled Steak with Anchovies

Preparation time: 25 minutes
Waiting time: 4 hours
Cooking time: 5-10 minutes

METRIC/IMPERIAL	AMERICAN
675–900 g/1½–2 lb beef steak	1½-2 lb beef steak
8 anchovy fillets	8 anchovy fillets
1 small onion	1 small onion
50 g/2 oz butter	4 tablespoons butter
grated rind and juice 1 lemon	grated rind and juice 1 lemon
2 tablespoons chopped parsley	2 tablespoons chopped parsley
2 tablespoons chopped thyme	2 tablespoons chopped thyme
1 tablespoon chopped marjoram	1 tablespoon chopped marjoram
6 sage leaves, chopped	6 sage leaves, chopped
freshly ground black pepper	freshly ground black pepper

Cut the steak into 4 even sized pieces.

Pound the anchovy fillets to a paste and chop the onion very finely so it is almost minced. Melt the butter in a frying pan on a low heat, taking care that it does not bubble. Stir in the anchovies, onion, lemon rind and juice and herbs. Season with the pepper. Brush the steak on both sides with the mixture. Leave it to marinate for at least 4 hours at room temperature.

Grill the steak to your liking.

Beef Teriyaki

Preparation time: 45 minutes
Waiting time: 2 hours
Cooking time: 15 minutes

METRIC/IMPERIAL	AMERICAN
675 g/1½ lb fillet steak	1½ lb fillet steak
marinade:	*marinade:*
4 tablespoons sherry	4 tablespoons sherry
6 tablespoons tamari, shoyu or soy sauce	⅜ cup tamari, shoyu or soy sauce
6 tablespoon chicken stock	⅜ cup chicken stock
4 spring onions, finely chopped	4 spring onions, finely chopped
½ teaspoon ground ginger	½ teaspoon ground ginger
1 garlic clove, crushed with a pinch sea salt	1 garlic clove, crushed with a pinch of sea salt
freshly ground black pepper	freshly ground black pepper
teriyaki sauce:	*teriyaki sauce:*
150 ml/¼ pint chicken stock	⅝ cup chicken stock
2 teaspoons arrowroot mixed with 2 tablespoons cold water	2 teaspoons arrowroot mixed with 2 tablespoons cold water
1 tablespoon dark Barbados sugar	1 tablespoon dark Barbados sugar

Cut the steak into twelve thin slices and lay them in a flat dish. To make the marinade, warm the sherry in an enamelled or stainless steel pan over a moderate heat. Ignite it and gently shake the pan until the flame dies. Stir in the tamari sauce and chicken stock and bring the mixture to the boil. Take it from the heat. Add the onions, ginger, garlic and pepper and cool to room temperature. Pour the marinade over the steak. Leave the steak for 2 hours at room temperature.

Lift out the steak. Strain the reserved marinade. Put it into a saucepan with the stock for the sauce. Bring it to the boil over a medium heat and then reduce the heat to a simmer. Stir in the arrowroot and the sugar. Cook, stirring, until the mixture thickens. Pour it into a bowl and cool it.

Heat a cast-iron grill (broiler) over a high heat. Dip the steak, one slice at a time, into the teriyaki sauce. Grill it for 1 minute on each side for rare, 1½–2 minutes on each side for well done.

No relishes are necessary.

Cheese-Topped Lamb

Preparation time: 10 minutes
Waiting time: nil
Cooking time: 8-14 minutes

METRIC/IMPERIAL	AMERICAN
4 large lamb chops	4 large lamb chops
4 tablespoons mushroom ketchup	4 tablespoons mushroom ketchup
4 tablespoons Worcestershire sauce	4 tablespoons Worcestershire sauce
2 tablespoons oil	2 tablespoons oil
100 g/4 oz Cheddar cheese, grated	1 cup grated Cheddar cheese

Trim the chops if necessary. Mix together 2 tablespoons each of the mushroom ketchup and Worcestershire sauce and all the oil.

Heat the grill. Brush half the sauce and oil mixture over one side of the chops. Lay the chops on the grill, sauce side down. Brush the remaining sauce mixture over the top of the chops.

Grill the chops until they are browned on one side. Turn them over and grill them until they are almost cooked through.

Cream together the cheese and the remaining ketchup and sauce. Press the mixture on top of the chops. Cook until the cheese is heated through and is beginning to melt.

Lamb Chops with Olive Mustard

Preparation time: 20 minutes
Waiting time: nil
Cooking time: 8 minutes

METRIC/IMPERIAL	AMERICAN
8 small lamb chops	8 small lamb chops
10 green olives	10 green olives
1 tablespoon capers	1 tablespoon capers
1 tablespoon Dijon mustard	1 tablespoon Dijon mustard

Stone and chop the olives. Chop the capers. Using a pestle and mortar, pound them together with the mustard until you have a smooth paste.

The chops are best cooked under a conventional grill (broiler) under a high heat. Grill the chops quite plainly, for 4 minutes on one side. Turn them over and grill them for 3 minutes. Spread them with the olive mustard and continue cooking for a further 1 minute.

Suggested relishes: Mushroom; Aubergine; Lemon and honey.

Lemon & Mustard Chops

Preparation time: 15 minutes
Waiting time: 1 hour
Cooking time: 8-14 minutes

METRIC/IMPERIAL	AMERICAN
8 small lamb chops	8 small lamb chops
2 tablespoons American mustard	2 tablespoons American mustard
juice 2 lemons	juice 2 lemons
4 tablespoons oil	¼ cup oil
4 tablespoons chopped parsley	¼ cup chopped parsley
4 large Hungarian gherkins	4 large Hungarian gherkins

Mix together the mustard, lemon juice, oil and parsley. Put the mixture into a flat dish. Put in the chops and turn them so they become well coated. Leave them for 1 hour at room temperature.

Grill the chops as above. Finely chop the gherkins. Serve them in a separate small dish in the same way as a relish.

Cumberland Chops

Preparation time: 20 minutes
Waiting time: 4 hours
Cooking time: 8-14 minutes

METRIC/IMPERIAL	AMERICAN
8 small lamb chops	8 small lamb chops
150 ml/¼ pint port (dry red wine may be used instead)	⅝ cup port (dry red wine may be used instead)
juice 1 large orange and grated rind of half, thinly pared rind half	juice 1 large orange and grated rind half, thinly pared rind half
2 tablespoons redcurrant jelly	2 tablespoons redcurrant jelly
2 tablespoons chopped chives	2 tablespoons chopped chives
2 tablespoons chopped mint	2 tablespoons chopped mint

Trim the chops if necessary. Put the port, orange juice and grated rind and redcurrant jelly into a saucepan and set them on a low heat for the jelly to melt. Cool them and pour them into a flat dish. Turn the chops in the mixture and leave them for at least 4 hours at room temperature, turning them several times.

Cut the thinly pared orange rind into thin strips. Blanch them for 2 minutes and drain them.

Heat a cast iron grill (broiler) on a high heat and grill (broil) the chops to your liking.

Serve them scattered with the strips of orange rind, chives and mint.

Pork Chops Grilled with Parmesan Cheese

Preparation time: 15 minutes
Waiting time: nil
Cooking time: 12-14 minutes

METRIC/IMPERIAL	AMERICAN
4 loin pork chops	4 loin pork chops
2 tablespoons tomato paste	2 tablespoons tomato paste
6 tablespoons dry white wine	⅜ cup dry white wine
2 teaspoons paprika	2 teaspoons paprika
¼ teaspoon cayenne pepper	¼ teaspoon cayenne pepper
8 sage leaves, chopped	8 sage leaves, chopped
45 g/1½ oz Parmesan cheese, grated	3 tablespoons grated Parmesan cheese

Cut the rind from the chops. Beat together the tomato paste, wine, paprika, cayenne pepper and sage. Heat a conventional grill (broiler) to high. Lay the chops on the hot rack and brush them with half the tomato mixture. Grill them until the top side browns (about 6 minutes).

Turn them over and brush them with the remaining tomato mixture. Grill the second side until it browns.

Scatter the cheese over the chops and put them back under the grill for it to melt.

From top to bottom:
Grilled Steak with Anchovies p. 39.
Steak with Orange p. 38.
Juniper Pork with Apples p. 46.
Cheese-Topped Lamb p. 41.

Opposite page 45:
Melted Cheese & Prawn Pittas p. 78.
Pizzas, clockwise from top:
Mushroom & Walnut Pizza p. 57.
Prawn & Red Pepper p. 53.
Lentil Pizza p. 56.
Anchovy Pizza p. 55.

Marinated Lombardy Pork

Preparation time: 20 minutes
Waiting time: 4 hours
Cooking time: 20 minutes

METRIC/IMPERIAL	AMERICAN
4 spare rib or loin pork chops	4 spare rib or loin pork chops
1 garlic clove, finely chopped	1 garlic clove, finely chopped
10 black peppercorns	10 black peppercorns
8 allspice berries	8 allspice berries
½ teaspoon sea salt	½ teaspoon sea salt
2 teaspoons mustard powder	2 teaspoons mustard powder
2 teaspoons honey	2 teaspoons honey
125 ml/4 fl oz dry white wine	½ cup dry white wine
125 ml/4 fl oz stock	½ cup stock
2 teaspoons chopped rosemary	2 teaspoons chopped rosemary

Trim the chops if neceesary. Crush the garlic, peppercorns, allspice and salt together and work them with the mustard powder and honey. Gradually mix in the wine and stock and add the rosemary. Put the marinade into a flat dish, big enough to take the chops without their overlapping.

Turn the pork in the marinade and leave it for at least 4 hours at room temperature, turning several times.

Heat a conventional grill (broiler) to high. Lay the pork on the hot rack and grill it close to the heat until it is a rich brown on both sides.

Remove the pork to a warm serving dish. Remove the grill rack and set the pan on top of the stove on a moderate heat. Pour in the marinade and bring it to the boil, stirring in any pieces of residue. Let the sauce simmer for 1 minute until it is a clear rich brown, and spoon it over the chops.

Note: if the sauce is not required, the chops may be cooked on a broiler or barbeque grill.

l

Juniper Pork with Apples

Preparation time: 20 minutes
Waiting time: nil
Cooking time: 14 minutes

METRIC/IMPERIAL	AMERICAN
4 loin pork chops	4 loin pork chops
12 juniper berries	12 juniper berries
6 blade peppercorns	6 blade peppercorns
pinch sea salt	pinch sea salt
1 garlic clove, finely chopped	1 garlic clove, finely chopped
4 sage leaves, finely chopped	4 sage leaves, finely chopped
2 crisp dessert apples	2 crisp dessert apples

Trim the rind and any excess fat from the chops. Using a pestle and mortar, crush together the juniper berries, peppercorns, salt, garlic and sage. Spread the mixture lightly over the chops.

Heat the grill (broiler) on a high heat. Put on the chops and brown them on each side. Lower the heat and cook the chops for about 7 minutes on each side or until they are cooked through. Remove them and keep them warm.

While the chops are cooking, core the apples and halve them lengthways. Cut the halves into slices about 5 mm/⅓ inch thick. Lay the apple slices on the griddle and cook them so they begin to brown on each side but remain firm.

Serve the chops with the apple slices on top.

Chinese Spare Ribs

Preparation time: 15 minutes
Waiting time: 2 hours
Cooking time: 30 minutes

METRIC/IMPERIAL
900 g/2 lb pork ribs
4 tablespoons tamari, soy or shoyu sauce
4 tablespoons dry sherry
½ teaspoon five-spice powder
½ teaspoon ground Szechuan or black pepper
pinch salt
1 tablespoon chilli sauce
15 g/½ oz fresh ginger root, peeled and grated

AMERICAN
2 lb pork spare ribs
¼ cup tamari, soy or shoyu sauce
¼ cup dry sherry
½ teaspoon five-spice powder
½ teaspoon ground Szechuan or black pepper
pinch salt
1 tablespoon chilli sauce
½ oz fresh ginger root, peeled and grated

Put the spare-ribs into a flat dish. Sprinkle them with half the sauce and sherry, the five-spice powder, pepper and salt. Leave them for 2 hours at room temperature. Grill them as above.

Mix together the remaining sauce and sherry, the chilli sauce and ginger root. Heat a wok or large frying pan on a high heat. Put in the spare ribs and pour in the sauce mixture. Stir-fry for 15 seconds. Lift the ribs immediately onto a serving dish.

Pineapple Spare Ribs

Preparation time: 15 minutes
Waiting time: 6-8 hours
Cooking time: 20 minutes

METRIC/IMPERIAL
900 g/2 lb pork ribs
150 ml/¼ pint natural pineapple juice
3 tablespoons tamari, shoyu or soy
sauce
8 spring onions, finely chopped
1 teaspoon ground ginger
1 garlic clove, crushed with a pinch of
salt

AMERICAN
2 lb pork spare ribs
⅝ cup natural pineapple juice
3 tablespoons tamari, shoyu or soy
sauce
8 spring onions, finely chopped
1 teaspoon ground ginger
1 garlic clove, crushed with a pinch of
salt

Put the spare ribs into a large, flat dish. Mix the rest of the ingredients together and pour them over the spare ribs. Leave them to marinate for 6–8 hours at room temperature, turning them once or twice.

Heat a conventional grill (broiler) to high. Lay the spare ribs on the hot rack and spoon the marinade over them. Grill them for about 20 minutes, turning them and basting them frequently until they are a good, rich brown all over.

PIZZA PARTY

Pizzas or, to use the correct Italian plural, pizze, were once made only around the Naples area of Italy and sold in the pizza house, known as pizzeria. The original pizza Napolitana was topped with tomatoes, herbs, anchovies, Mozarella cheese made from Buffalos milk and black olives. It was good hearty fare and one pizza was cut into wedges to serve four or more people who washed it down with a glass of rough red wine.

Gradually this open pie, which is really what 'pizza' means, spread throughout Italy and each region developed it's own favourite topping. A Roman pizza, for example, had onions softened in olive oil in place of the tomato; a Ligurian pizza had both. A topping for a pizza Francescana included mushrooms and ham; and on a pizza con cozze the anchovies were replaced by fresh mussels.

When pizze were made at home instead of the pizzeria, the yeast dough base was often replaced by pastry. Small pizze, known as pizette, were made, each one a complete individual portion. The pizza al tegame was made completely in a frying pan; and others were made in tart dishes to make them more substantial, one example being the pizza rustica which contained a mixture of bechamel sauce, ham, cheese and eggs.

The more the pizza spread across the world, the more varied the fillings and toppings became. Now, almost anything goes. Cheese, meat, fish, nuts, pulses, even eggs can top a pizza. Turn out your store cupboard and see what you have. Making a pizza is an excellent way of using up small quantities of ingredients. The only rules are that the final topping should not be too liquid or too dry and chunky. When you have exhausted all the savoury possibilities, you can then serve a pizza as a sweet.

A pizza base can be made from a soft yeast dough or from a more quickly prepared scone-type mixture. Bake it in the oven or fry it in the pan. Whichever method that you choose, always use wholewheat flour. Then you will have a meal that is both nutritious and well balanced besides being colourful, substantial and good to eat.

A flat 25 cm/10 inch pizza with a base made with 225 g/8 oz/2 cups wholewheat flour will serve four people as a main meal. A deep dish pizza of the same diameter and made with the same amount of flour should serve six. The same amount of dough will make two 20 cm/8 inch pizzas or four 15 cm/6 inch pizzas. For a sweet pizza, use half the amount of dough.

This should only be a sweet treat at the end of the meal, and not a main course so you therefore need less.

The times for preparation, waiting and cooking in these recipes do not include the time needed to make the dough.

Pizza in the Pan

Preparation time: 15 minutes
Waiting time: nil
Cooking time: 10-12 minutes

METRIC/IMPERIAL	AMERICAN
225 g/8 oz wholewheat flour	2 cups wholewheat flour
½ teaspoon fine sea salt	½ teaspoon fine sea salt
½ teaspoon bicarbonate of soda	½ teaspoon bicarbonate of soda
4 tablespoons natural yoghurt	4 tablespoons natural yoghurt
4 tablespoons water	¼ cup water
7 tablespoons olive oil	½ cup olive oil

Put the flour, salt and soda into a bowl. Make a well in the centre and put in the yoghurt, water and 4 tablespoons olive oil. Mix everything to a dough. Turn it onto a floured board and knead it lightly until it is smooth. Roll out the dough to a size just larger than a 25 cm/10 inch diameter frying pan.

Heat the remaining oil in a 25 cm/10 inch diameter frying pan on a low heat. Put in the rolled dough, pressing the edges to make them slightly thicker than the middle. Cook for about 5 minutes so the underside browns. Turn the dough and immediately put on the prepared topping.

If a cheese topping needs to be melted, cover the pan and it will melt as the base finishes cooking. If the topping has to be browned, continue cooking uncovered until the base is cooked. Then put the pan under a preheated high grill.

This base can be prepared in advance. It can also be cooked, frozen, thawed at room temperature when needed and heated through on a low heat.

Yeast Dough for Pizzas

Preparation time: 30 minutes
Waiting time: 1 hour
Cooking time: 10-15 minutes

METRIC/IMPERIAL	AMERICAN
15 g/½ oz fresh yeast or 2 teaspoons dried	½ oz fresh yeast or 2 teaspoons dried
½ teaspoon honey	½ teaspoon honey
90 ml/3 fl oz warm water	⅜ cup warm water
225 g/8 oz wholewheat flour	2 cups wholewheat flour
½ teaspoon fine sea salt	½ teaspoon fine sea salt
1 egg, beaten	1 egg, beaten
1 tablespoon olive oil	1 tablespoon olive oil

If using fresh yeast, cream it with the honey and mix in the water. If dried, dissolve the honey in the water and sprinkle the yeast on top. Leave the yeast in a warm place to froth, about 10 minutes for fresh yeast, 20-30 minutes for dried.

Put the flour and salt into a bowl. Make a well in the centre. Mix in the yeast mixture and oil. Turn the dough onto a floured board and knead it. Put it back into the bowl, cover it with a clean tea towel and leave it in a warm place for 1 hour or until doubled in size.

Heat the oven to 200C/400F/gas 6. Knead the dough again. This amount of dough will make one 25 cm/10 inch flat pizza or one 25 cm/10 inch deep dish pizza. It will also make two 20 cm/8 inch pizzas or four 15 cm/6 inch pizzas.

For a flat pizza, roll out the dough to the required size, turning over the edges to thicken them. Prick the base all over with a fork. Lay the topping on the rolled dough and leave for 10 minutes. Bake for 25 minutes.

If the recipe requires the base to be baked blind, use something heavy to weight it down such as pearl barley or rice. Bake for 10–15 minutes, depending on the final topping. Cool it slightly. Put on the topping and bake again.

For a deep dish pizza, roll out the dough as for pastry. Roll it round the rolling pin and carefully lower it into a flan tin or dish. Ease the edges into the corners. Prick the base all over with a fork. Again, to bake blind, make sure the base is well filled with pearl barley or small beans.

A part cooked pizza base can be kept in the refrigerator for up to two days. It can also be frozen and thawed at room temperature before the topping is added.

Quick Pizza Dough

Preparation time: 20 minutes
Waiting time: nil
Cooking time: 10-15 minutes

METRIC/IMPERIAL	AMERICAN
225 g/8 oz wholewheat flour	2 cups wholewheat flour
1 teaspoon fine sea salt	1 teaspoon fine sea salt
1 teaspoon bicarbonate of soda	1 teaspoon bicarbonate of soda
3 tablespoons olive oil	3 tablespoons olive oil
150 ml/¼ pint natural yoghurt	⅝ cup natural yoghurt

Put the flour into a bowl with the salt and bicarbonate of soda. Make a well in the centre and add the oil and yoghurt. Mix everything to a dough. Turn it onto a floured work surface and knead it lightly until it is smooth.

This will make one 25 cm/10 inch pizza, two 20 cm/8 inch pizzas or four 15 cm/6 inch pizzas. Line the pizza tins and prick the dough all over with a fork.

Depending on the filling the dough can either be cooked with the filling on top or it can be baked blind for a short time first. Make sure it is well weighted down with pearl barley or small beans.

This quick base can be stored or frozen in the same way as the yeast base.

Prawn (Shrimp) & Red Pepper Pizza

Preparation time: 30 minutes
Waiting time: nil
Cooking time: 10 minutes

METRIC/IMPERIAL	AMERICAN
pizza dough made with 225 g/8 oz wholewheat flour	pizza dough made with 2 cups wholewheat flour
2 red peppers	2 sweet red peppers
225 g/8 oz tomatoes	½ lb tomatoes
3 tablespoons oil	3 tablespoons oil
1 large onion, finely chopped	1 large onion, finely chopped
1 garlic clove, finely chopped	1 garlic clove, finely chopped
1 teaspoon paprika	1 teaspoon paprika
¼ teaspoon cayenne pepper	¼ teaspoon cayenne pepper
100 g/4 oz shelled prawns	1 cup shelled shrimp
175 g/6 oz Mozarella cheese	6 oz Mozarella cheese

Heat the oven to 200C/400F/gas 6. Roll out the dough to make a 25 cm/10 inch pizza. Bake it blind for 10 minutes.

Core and seed the peppers. Finely chop one and a half. Scald, skin and chop the tomatoes. Heat the oil in a frying pan on a low heat. Put in the onion and garlic and cook them for 2 minutes. Mix in the chopped peppers and cook until the onion is very soft and beginning to change colour. Mix in the tomatoes, paprika and cayenne pepper. Cook gently for 5 minutes. Take the pan from the heat and mix in the prawns (shrimp).

Spread the mixture over the pizza base. Thinly slice the cheese and lay it over the top. Cut the remaining half pepper into thin strips and use them as a garnish. Bake the pizza for a further 10 minutes.

Egg & Corn Pizzette

Preparation time: 30 minutes
Waiting time: nil
Cooking time: 10 minutes

METRIC/IMPERIAL	AMERICAN
pizza dough, either yeast or quick, made with 225 g/8 oz wholewheat flour	pizza dough made with 2 cups wholewheat flour
3 tablespoons oil	3 tablespoons oil
1 medium onion, finely chopped	1 medium onion, finely chopped
4 lean back bacon rashers, finely chopped	4 lean back bacon rashers, finely chopped
1 garlic clove, finely chopped	1 garlic clove, finely chopped
1 red pepper, cored, seeded and chopped	1 sweet red pepper, cored, seeded and chopped
225 g/8 oz tomatoes, finely chopped	½ lb tomatoes, finely chopped
1 teaspoon paprika	1 teaspoon paprika
pinch cayenne pepper	pinch cayenne pepper
one 175 g/6 oz tin sweetcorn, drained	one 6 oz tin sweetcorn, drained
4 eggs	4 eggs
50 g/2 oz Cheddar cheese, grated	½ cup grated Cheddar cheese

Heat the oven to 200C/400F/gas 6. Roll the dough to make four individual pizzas. Lay them on floured baking sheets, prick them with a fork and bake them blind for 10 minutes.

Heat the oil in a frying pan on a low heat. Mix in the onion, bacon, garlic and pepper and cook them until the onion is soft. Add the tomatoes, paprika, cayenne pepper and sweetcorn and cook them for a further 2 minutes. Cool the mixture slightly.

Divide the mixture between the pizza bases. Make a hole in the centre of the mixture to take the egg yolk and carefully break the eggs on top.

Scatter the cheese over the yolks. Bake the pizzas for a further 10 minutes.

Anchovy Pizza

Preparation time: 30 minutes
Waiting time: nil
Cooking time: 10 minutes

METRIC/IMPERIAL	AMERICAN
pizza dough made with 225 g/8 oz wholewheat flour	pizza dough made with 2 cups wholewheat flour
one 40 g/1½ oz tin anchovy fillets	one 1½ oz tin anchovy fillets
2 green peppers	2 sweet green peppers
2 large onions	2 large onions
4 tablespoons olive oil	4 tablespoons olive oil
2 garlic cloves, finely chopped	2 garlic cloves, finely chopped
10 black olives	10 black olives
225 g/8 oz Mozarella cheese	½ lb Mozarella cheese
4 tomatoes	4 tomatoes

Heat the oven to 200C/400F/gas 6. Roll out the dough and line a 25 cm/10 inch diameter pizza plate. Prick it all over with a fork and bake it blind for 15 minutes.

Finely chop the anchovies. Core and seed the peppers and cut them into 2.5 cm/1 inch strips. Halve and thinly slice the onions. Heat the oil in a large frying pan on a low heat. Put in the onions and garlic and soften them. Mix in the peppers and continue cooking, stirring frequently, until the onions are golden and the peppers beginning to soften. Take the pan from the heat.

Stone and chop the olives. Mix these and the anchovies into the peppers and onions. Spread the mixture over the pizza base. Thinly slice the cheese and lay it over the top. Thinly slice the tomatoes and make a pattern with the slices over the cheese. Return the pizza to the oven for a further 10 minutes for the cheese to melt.

Lentil Pizza

Preparation time: 1½ hours
Waiting time: nil
Cooking time: 10 minutes

METRIC/IMPERIAL	AMERICAN
pizza dough made with 225 g/8 oz wholewheat flour	pizza dough made with 2 cups wholewheat flour
100 g/4 oz green lentils	½ cup green lentils
one 400 g/14 oz tin tomatoes in juice	one 14 oz tin tomatoes in juice
2 tablespoons chopped thyme	2 tablespoons chopped thyme
2 tablespoons chopped marjoram	2 tablespoons chopped marjoram
225 g/8 oz aubergine	½ lb egg plant
1 tablespoon sea salt	1 tablespoon sea salt
1 small red pepper	1 small sweet red pepper
1 small green pepper	1 small sweet green pepper
1 medium onion	1 medium onion
2 tablespoons oil	2 tablespoons oil
1 garlic clove, finely chopped	1 garlic clove, finely chopped
100 g/4 oz Cheddar cheese, grated	1 cup grated Cheddar cheese
4 black olives	4 black olives

Roll out the dough and line a 25 cm/10 inch pizza or tart tin. Prick it all over with a fork and bake it blind for 15 minutes. Put the lentils, tomatoes and herbs into a saucepan. Bring them to the boil, cover and simmer them for 50 minutes, or until the lentils are soft.

Finely dice the aubergine (egg plant). Put it into a collander and sprinkle it with the salt. Leave it to drain for 15 minutes. Rinse it with cold water and dry it with kitchen paper. Core, seed and finely chop the peppers. Finely chop the onion.

Heat the oil in a frying pan on a low heat. Mix in the aubergine (egg plant), peppers, onion and garlic and cook them gently, stirring occasionally, until all are soft, about 15 minutes. Mix them into the cooked lentils.

Spread the lentil mixture over the pizza base. Scatter the cheese over the top. Halve and stone the olives and use them as a garnish. Return the pizza to the oven for 10 minutes for the cheese to melt.

Mushroom & Walnut Pizza

Preparation time: 30 minutes
Waiting time: nil
Cooking time: 10 minutes

METRIC/IMPERIAL	AMERICAN
pizza dough made with 225 g/8 oz wholewheat flour	pizza dough made with 2 cups wholewheat flour
175 g/6 oz button mushrooms	6 oz button mushrooms
25 g/1 oz shelled walnuts	⅛ cup shelled walnut meats
25 g/1 oz butter	2 tablespoons butter
1 small onion, thinly sliced	1 small onion, thinly sliced
2 tablespoons wholewheat flour	2 tablespoons wholewheat flour
225 ml/8 fl oz milk	1 cup milk
3 tablespoons chopped parsley	3 tablespoons chopped parsley
1 tablespoon chopped thyme	1 tablespoon chopped thyme
sea salt and freshly ground black pepper	sea salt and freshly ground black pepper
100 g/4 oz Edam cheese, grated	1 cup grated Edam cheese

Heat the oven to 200C/400F/gas 6. Roll out the dough and line a 25 cm/10 inch pizza tin or tart tin. Bake the base blind for 15 minutes.

Thinly slice the mushrooms and finely chop the walnuts. Melt the butter in a saucepan on a low heat. Stir in the onion and soften it. Stir in the mushrooms, cover and cook gently for 5 minutes. Take out about 15 g/½ oz of the mushrooms and reserve them for a garnish.

Stir in the flour and then the milk into the rest. Bring the milk to the boil, stirring. Stir in the herbs and seasonings. Take the pan from the heat and mix in half the cheese and half the walnuts.

Spread the filling over the pizza base. Scatter the remaining cheese and then the remaining mushrooms over the top. Garnish with the reserved mushroom slices.

Bake the pizza for a further 10 minutes.

Deep Dish Ham Pizza

Preparation time: 45 minutes
Waiting time: nil
Cooking time: 10 minutes

METRIC/IMPERIAL	AMERICAN
pizza dough made with 225 g/8 oz wholewheat flour	pizza dough made with 2 cups wholewheat flour
225 g/8 oz aubergines	½ lb egg plant
1 tablespoon fine sea salt	1 tablespoon fine sea salt
100 g/4 oz cooked lean ham	¼ lb cooked lean ham
450 g/1 lb courgettes	1 lb zucchini
1 green pepper	1 sweet green pepper
4 tablespoons oil	¼ cup oil
1 large onion, finely chopped	1 large onion, finely chopped
1 garlic clove, finely chopped	1 garlic clove, finely chopped
150 ml/¼ pint tomato juice	⅝ cup tomato juice
2 tablespoons chopped thyme	2 tablespoons chopped thyme
75 g/3 oz Cheddar cheese, grated	¾ cup grated Cheddar cheese
10 black olives, halved and stoned	10 black olives, halved and stoned

Heat the oven to 200C/400F/gas 6. Roll out the dough to line a 25 cm/10 inch dish or tin, 2.5 cm/1 inch deep. Bake it blind for 10 minutes.

Finely chop the aubergines (egg plant). Put them into a collander and sprinkle them with the salt. Leave them to drain for 20 minutes. Rinse them with cold water and dry them with kitchen paper. Finely chop the ham and the courgettes (zucchini). Core, seed and finely chop the pepper.

Heat the oil in a large frying pan on a low heat. Put in the onion and garlic and cook them for 2 minutes. Mix in the aubergines (egg plant), courgettes (zucchini) and pepper. Cook gently, stirring frequently, for 5 minutes. Pour in the tomato juice and bring it to the boil. Add the thyme. Cover and simmer for 10 minutes. Take the pan from the heat and mix in the ham.

Put the mixture into the baked shell. Scatter the cheese over the top and garnish with the olive halves. Bake the pizza for a further 10 minutes.

Deep Dish Sausage & Cheese Pizza

Preparation time: 45 minutes
Waiting time: nil
Cooking time: 20 minutes

METRIC/IMPERIAL	AMERICAN
pizza dough made with 225 g/8 oz wholewheat flour	pizza dough made with 2 cups wholewheat flour
300 g/10 oz aubergines	10 oz egg plant
1 tablespoon sea salt	1 tablespoon sea salt
1 red pepper	1 sweet red pepper
1 green pepper	1 sweet green pepper
6 tablespoons olive oil	⅜ cup olive oil
1 large onion quartered and thinly sliced	1 large onion, quartered and thinly sliced
1 garlic clove, finely chopped	1 garlic clove, finely chopped
one 225 g/8 oz boiling sausage	one ½ lb boiling sausage
225 g/8 oz tomatoes	½ lb tomatoes
100 g/4 oz Bel Paese cheese	¼ lb Bel Paese cheese
100 g/4 oz Cheddar cheese, grated	1 cup grated Cheddar cheese

Heat the oven to 200C/400F/gas 6. Roll out the dough and use it to line a deep, 25 cm/10 inch pizza dish or tart tin. Bake it blind for 10 minutes.

Cut the aubergines (egg plants) into 1 cm/⅜ inch slices. Put them into a collander and sprinkle them with the salt. Leave them to drain for 20 minutes. Rinse them with cold water and dry them with kitchen paper.

Core and seed the peppers and cut them into 2.5 cm/1 inch strips. Heat half the oil in a frying pan on a low heat. Mix in the peppers, onion and garlic and cook them until the onion is soft. Remove them.

Add the remaining oil to the pan. Put in the aubergine (egg plant) slices and brown them lightly on each side. Remove them. Thinly slice the sausage, the tomatoes and the Bel Paese cheese.

Put the aubergine (egg plant) slices in the bottom of the pizza shell and top them with the Bel Paese cheese. Put in the peppers and onion and then the sausage slices. Top these with the tomato slices and cover them with the Cheddar cheese.

Bake the pizza for a further 20 minutes or until the Cheddar cheese has melted and is beginning to brown.

Summer-Time Deep Dish Pizza

Preparation time: 50 minutes
Waiting time: nil
Cooking time: 10 minutes

METRIC/IMPERIAL	AMERICAN
pizza dough made with 225 g/8 oz wholewheat flour	pizza dough made with 2 cups wholewheat flour
225 g/8 oz shelled peas	½ lb shelled peas
225 g/8 oz shelled broad beans	½ lb shelled broad beans
25 g/1 oz butter	1 oz butter
2 tablespoons wholewheat flour	2 tablespoons wholewheat flour
225 ml/8 fl oz milk	1 cup milk
100 g/4 oz quark or other low fat soft cheese	¼ lb quark or other low fat soft cheese
½ oz Parmesan cheese, grated	1 tablespoon Parmesan cheese, grated
4 tablespoon chopped parsley	¼ cup chopped parsley
sea salt and freshly ground black pepper 4 eggs, hard boiled	sea salt and freshly ground black pepper
225 g/8 oz Bel Paese cheese	4 hard cooked eggs
	½ lb Bel Paese cheese

Heat the oven to 200C/400F/gas 6. Roll out the dough and use it to line a deep 25 cm/10 inch pizza tin or tart tin. Prick it all over with a fork and bake it blind for 15 minutes.

Cook the peas and beans together in lightly salted water until tender. Drain them. Melt the butter in a saucepan on a low heat. Stir in the flour and then the milk. Take the pan from the heat. Put the quark into a bowl and gradually beat in the milk sauce.

Add the Parmesan, parsley and seasonings. Finely chop the eggs and fold them in with the peas and beans.

Put the mixture into the pizza case. Thinly slice the cheese and lay it over the top. Return the pizza to the oven for 10 minutes for the cheese to soften and begin to melt.

Top: Tuna Pan Pizza p. 62.
Bottom: Deep Dish Ham Pizza p. 58

Courgette (Zucchini) Pan Pizza

Preparation time: 30 minutes
Waiting time: nil
Cooking time: 10 minutes

METRIC/IMPERIAL	AMERICAN
base for pan pizza made with 225 g/8 oz wholewheat flour	base for pan pizza made with 2 cups wholewheat flour
350 g/12 oz courgettes	¼ lb zucchini
225 g/8 oz tomatoes	½ lb tomatoes
3 tablespoons oil	3 tablespoons oil
1 medium onion, thinly sliced	1 medium onion, thinly sliced
1 garlic clove, thinly sliced	1 garlic clove, thinly sliced
2 tablespoons chopped parsley	2 tablespoons chopped parsley
15 g/½ oz Parmesan cheese, grated	1 tablespoon grated Parmesan cheese
175 g/6 oz Mozarella cheese, thinly sliced	6 oz Mozarella cheese, thinly sliced
10 black olives, halved and stoned	10 black olives, halved and stoned

Thinly slice the courgettes (zucchini) and tomatoes. Heat the oil in a frying pan on a low heat. Put in the onion and garlic and soften them. Mix in the courgettes (zucchini) and cook them for about 10 minutes so they are tender but not soggy.

Cook the pizza dough on one side as above. Turn it over and scatter it with parsley. Put on the courgettes and onions and scatter them with the Parmesan cheese. Lay the tomato slices on top and then the slices of Mozarella. Garnish with the olive halves.

Cover the pan and cook for a further 5 minutes so the dough is cooked and the cheese beginning to melt.

Clockwise from top left:
Tuna & Lemon Pittas p. 74.
Avocado Salad Pittas p. 76.
Red Bean & Cheese Pittas p. 73.
Spiced Chickpea Pittas p. 72.
Lamb & Lemon Pittas p. 68.

Tuna Pan Pizza

Preparation time: 20 minutes
Waiting time: nil
Cooking time: 15 minutes

METRIC/IMPERIAL	AMERICAN
base for pan pizza made with	base for pan pizza made with 2 cups
225 g/8 oz wholewheat flour	wholewheat flour
one 200 g/7 oz tin tuna fish	one 7 oz tin tuna fish
225 g/8 oz tomatoes	½ lb tomatoes
1 garlic clove, crushed	1 garlic clove, crushed
2 tablespoons tomato paste	2 tablespoons tomato paste
4 tablespoons chopped parsley	¼ cup chopped parsley
1 tablespoon chopped basil (or 1	1 tablespoon chopped basil (or 1
teaspoon dried)	teaspoon dried)
grated rind 1 lemon	grated rind 1 lemon
6 black olives, stoned and finely	6 black olives, stoned and finely
chopped	chopped
pinch cayenne pepper	pinch cayenne pepper
175 g/6 oz Mozarella cheese, thinly	6 oz Mozarella cheese, thinly sliced
sliced	4 anchovy fillets, halved lengthways
4 anchovy fillets, halved lengthways	

Drain and flake the tuna. Scald, skin and chop the tomatoes. Mix together the tuna, tomatoes, garlic, tomato paste, herbs, lemon rind, olives and cayenne pepper.

Cook the pizza dough on one side as above. Turn it over and spread it with the tuna mixture. Lay the cheese over the top and decorate with the strips of anchovy.

Cover the pan and cook the pizza for a further 10 minutes so the dough is cooked and the cheese beginning to melt.

Apple & Yoghurt Pizza

Preparation time: 30 minutes
Waiting time: nil
Cooking time: 15 minutes

METRIC/IMPERIAL	AMERICAN
pizza dough made with 100 g/4 oz wholewheat flour	pizza dough made with 1 cup wholewheat flour
2 dessert apples	2 dessert apples
2 tablespoons clear honey	2 tablespoons clear honey
1 teaspoon ground cinnamon	1 teaspoon ground cinnamon
1 egg beaten	1 egg beaten
90 ml/3 fl oz natural yoghurt	⅜ cup natural yoghurt

Heat the oven to 200C/400F/gas 6. Roll out the dough and line a 20 cm/8 inch pizza or tart tin. Prick it all over with a fork and bake it blind for 10 minutes.

Peel and core the apples and cut them into lengthways slices. Put them into a bowl and gently fold in the honey and cinnamon. Arrange the apple slices attractively on the pizza base.

Beat the egg and gradually beat in the yoghurt. Pour the mixture over the apples. Return the pizza to the oven for 15 minutes, or until the yoghurt is just beginning to colour.

Banana & Dried Fruit Pizza

Preparation time: 45 minutes
Waiting time: nil
Cooking time: 15 minutes

METRIC/IMPERIAL	AMERICAN
pizza dough made with 100 g/4 oz wholewheat flour	pizza dough made with 1 cup wholewheat flour
50 g/2 oz dried apricots	2 oz dried apricots
150 ml/¼ pint orange juice	⅝ cup orange juice
2 bananas	2 bananas
50 g/2 oz sultanas	⅓ cup sultanas
50 g/2 oz raisins	⅓ cup raisins
15 g/½ ox flaked almonds	1 tablespoon flaked almonds
1 tablespoon honey, melted	1 tablespoon honey, melted

Heat the oven to 200C/400F/gas 6. Roll out the dough and line a 20 cm/8 inch diameter pizza tin or sponge tin. Bake it blind for 10 minutes.

Put the apricots into a saucepan with the orange juice. Bring them to the boil and simmer them for 20 minutes. Drain them. Liquidise the apricots with 1½ bananas. Mix them with the sultanas and raisins.

Spread the fruit mixture over the pizza base. Thinly slice the remaining half banana and arrange the slices on the top. Scatter the flaked almonds in between. Brush the banana slices with the melted honey.

Bake the pizza for a further 15 minutes. It can be served hot or cold.

Nutty Plum Pizza

Preparation time: 30 minutes
Waiting time: nil
Cooking time: 10 minutes

METRIC/IMPERIAL	AMERICAN
pizza base made with 125 g/4 oz wholewheat flour	pizza base made with 1 cup wholewheat flour
75 g/3 oz shelled mixed nuts	¾ cup shelled mixed nuts
4 tablespoons natural yoghurt	¼ cup natural yoghurt
½ teaspoon ground mixed spice	½ teaspoon ground mixed spice
225 g/8 oz dark cooking plums	½ lb dark cooking plums
50 g/2 oz honey	1 cup honey
10 blanched almonds	10 blanched almonds

Heat the oven to 200C/400F/gas 6. Roll the dough into a 20 cm/8 inch round. Lay it on a floured baking sheet. Prick it all over with a fork and bake it blind for 10 minutes. Cool it.

Grind the nuts in a liquidiser or grinder. Mix them with the ground mixed spice and the yoghurt. Spread the mixture over the pizza base.

Stone and slice the plums. Put the honey into a saucepan and set it on a low heat to melt. Take the pan from the heat and gently fold in the sliced plums.

Spoon them onto the nut base. Garnish with the blanched almonds. Bake the pizza for a further 10 minutes. Serve it hot.

PITTA PACKETS

Pittas, the oval, bread pockets that came originally from the Middle East and Greece, have become very popular in the West in recent years. We have been largely introduced to them by the ever-increasing numbers of take-away kebab houses where they are usually filled with pieces of skewered and grilled lamb topped with raw onion, tomato and a wedge of lemon. They make a delicious, easy to eat and completely balanced meal.

In their countries of origin, pittas are used as holders for all kinds of food. Lamb, either minced or in cubes, is the most used meat; and there are numerous vegetarian fillings such as el ful, a brown bean and egg salad from Egypt; spiced balls of mashed chickpeas known as felafel from Israel; and the small balls of goats cheese preserved in olive oil that are known as labneh. Fried or grilled cheese is another popular filling; and fish, either hot or cold, can also be used. Salads made with olives, avocados and all types of cooked beans and lentils have all been used to fill a pitta.

Besides being convenient holders for food, pittas can also be torn like a bread roll and used to scoop up dips such as taramasalata, made from smoked cod's roe and the delicious chickpea, tahini and lemon mixture known as hummus. A pitta can accompany a salad with a large amount of rich dressing or a meat dish with a thick sauce.

Both white and wholemeal pittas are readily available from specialist shops and supermarkets. Both are easy to make. If you can make a plain loaf, you can easily make pitta breads.

If a pitta is filled with a simple green or mixed vegetable salad it can make a tasty snack for the lunch box or the quick lunch at home. Add beans, cheese, eggs or cold meats to the filling and it becomes a more substantial lunch or supper dish. If a hot dish is cooked specially for the pitta, then you have a tasty main meal that can be served to both family and friends.

Why not have a pitta party? On the table, put a selection of diced salad vegetables, dishes of cooked beans, diced cheese, flaked fish, chopped nuts, olives, and several bowls of different dressings. In a basket put a big pile of wholewheat pitta bread. Then everyone can help themselves and fill the pittas as they please.

Wholewheat Pitta Bread

Preparation time: 45 minutes
Waiting time: 1 hour 20 minutes
Cooking time: 15 minutes

METRIC/IMPERIAL	AMERICAN
450 g/1 lb wholewheat flour	4 cups wholewheat flour
25 g/1 oz fresh yeast or	1 oz fresh yeast or
15 g/½ oz dried	½ oz dried
1 teaspoon honey	1 teaspoon honey
275 ml/½ pint warm water	1¼ cups warm water
2 teaspoons sea salt	2 teaspoons sea salt

Put the flour into a bowl. Cream the yeast with the honey and half the water and leave it in a warm place until it begins to froth, about 10 minutes for fresh yeast, 20-30 minutes for dried. Dissolve the salt in the remaining water.

Make a well in the flour. Mix in the yeast and then the salt water. Mix everything to a dough. Cover it with a clean towel and leave it in a warm place for 1 hour or until doubled in size.

Heat the oven to 230C/450F/gas 8. Divide the dough into six pieces and roll each one into an oval about 12 × 20 cm/5 × 8 inches and 6 mm/¼ inch thick. Put them onto a floured board or baking sheet, cover them with the tea towel again and leave them in a warm place for 20 minutes.

Flour one large or two small baking sheets. Put them into the oven to become really hot. Lay the pittas on the hot baking sheets and bake them for 15 minutes so they are just beginning to brown.

If the pittas are to be served hot immediately, wrap them in a clean, thick napkin to keep them warm. They can also be cooled completely on a wire rack, if they are to be served with cold fillings.

Storing

Pittas keep best if they are put into the refrigerator in a plastic bag. They should stay fresh for up to four days. Put them either under the grill or in the oven for a short time if you wish to serve them hot or warm.

If you batchbake or need to keep even a smaller number of pittas for longer than this, store them in two's in plastic bags in the freezer. Thaw them by putting them directly into a hot oven for 10 minutes or into the microwave on a high setting for 2 minutes.

Lamb & Lemon Pittas

Preparation time: 30 minutes
Waiting time: 4 hours
Cooking time: 15 minutes

METRIC/IMPERIAL	AMERICAN
one half shoulder lamb	one half shoulder lamb
4 tablespoons olive oil	¼ cup olive oil
grated rind and juice 1 lemon	grated rind and juice 1 lemon
1 tablespoon chopped lemon thyme	1 tablespoon chopped lemon thyme
(use ordinary thyme if lemon thyme is	(use ordinary thyme if lemon thyme is
not available)	not available)
2 tablespoons chopped parsley	2 tablespoons chopped parsley
1 garlic clove, crushed with a pinch sea	1 garlic clove, crushed with a pinch sea
salt	salt
freshly ground black pepper	freshly ground black pepper
serving:	*serving:*
20 black olives, halved and stoned	20 black olives, halved and stoned
1 large onion, finely chopped	1 large onion, finely chopped
4 small, very fresh courgettes, finely	4 small, very fresh zucchini, finely
chopped	chopped
2 green peppers, finely chopped	2 sweet green peppers, finely
25 g/1 oz parsley, chopped	chopped
	½ cup chopped parsley

Bone the lamb. Discard any excess fat. Cut the lean into 2.5 cm/1 inch cubes. Beat the marinade ingredients together. Mix in the lamb and leave it at room temperature for 4 hours. Thread the cubes onto four kebab skewers.

Heat the grill to high. Grill the kebabs as close to the heat as possible until they are browned all over and cooked through, about 15 minutes.

Serve the kebabs with hot pittas and have the olives, onion, courgettes, peppers and parsley in separate bowls.

Minced Lamb Pittas

Preparation time: 15 minutes
Waiting time: nil
Cooking time: 15 minutes

METRIC/IMPERIAL	AMERICAN
450 g/1 lb minced lamb	1 lb ground lamb
2 green peppers	2 sweet green peppers
5 red or green chillis	5 red or green chillis
3 tablespoons oil	3 tablespoons oil
1 medium onion, finely chopped	1 medium onion, finely chopped
1 garlic clove, finely chopped	1 garlic clove, finely chopped
1 teaspoon paprika	1 teaspoon paprkia
1 teaspoon ground cumin	1 teaspoon ground cumin
1 teaspoon ground coriander	1 teaspoon ground coriander
juice ½ lemon	juice ½ lemon

Core, seed and finely chop the peppers and chillis. Heat the oil in a frying pan on a high heat. Put in the lamb and brown it. Mix in the peppers, chillis, onion, garlic and spices. Lower the heat and stir for 2 minutes. Add the lemon juice, cover and cook gently for 15 minutes, stirring occasionally. The mixture should be quite dry.

Put the lamb into warmed pittas. A side salad is the best accompaniment.

Pork Pittas

Preparation time: 30 minutes
Waiting time: 4 hours
Cooking time: 15 minutes

METRIC/IMPERIAL	AMERICAN
675 g/1½ lb lean port, shoulder, hand or spare rib	1½ lean pork, shoulder, hand or spare rib
marinade:	*marinade:*
1 teaspoon mustard powder	1 teaspoon mustard powder
1 teaspoon clear honey	1 teaspoon clear honey
2 tablespoons dry white wine	2 tablespoons dry white wine
1 tablespoon oil	1 tablespoon oil
1 garlic clove, crushed with a pinch of salt	1 garlic clove crushed with a pinch sea salt
½ teaspoon black peppercorns, coarsely crushed	½ teaspoon black peppercorns, coarsely crushed
2 teaspoons chopped rosemary	2 teaspoons chopped rosemary
2 teaspoons chopped sage	2 teaspoons chopped sage
for serving:	*for serving:*
1 large onion, quartered and thinly sliced	1 large onion, quartered and thinly sliced
8 celery sticks, chopped	8 celery sticks, chopped

Cut the pork into pieces 2.5 cm/1 inch square and 1.5 cm/½ inch thick. Thread them onto four kebab skewers. Lay them on a long, flat dish.

Put the mustard into a bowl and work in first the honey and then the wine and oil. Mix in the garlic, peppercorns, rosemary and sage. Brush the marinade over the kebabs. Leave the kebabs to stand at room temperature for 4 hours.

Heat the grill to high. Lay the kebabs on the hot rack and baste them with the marinade that has collected in the dish. Grill them on all sides, as close to the heat as possible, until they are browned all over and cooked through, about 15 minutes.

Serve the kebabs with hot pittas. Hand the onion and celery separately.

Vegetable Kebab & Cheese Pittas

Preparation time: 30 minutes
Waiting time: 20 minutes
Cooking time: 10 minutes

METRIC/IMPERIAL	AMERICAN
225 g/8 oz aubergine	½ lb egg plant
1 tablespoon sea salt	1 tablespoon sea salt
225 g/8 oz courgettes	½ lb zucchini
4 tablespoons olive oil	¼ cup olive oil
juice ½ lemon	juice ½ lemon
1 garlic clove, crushed with a pinch sea salt	1 garlic clove, crushed with a pinch sea salt
freshly ground black pepper	freshly ground black pepper
freshly grated nutmeg	freshly grated nutmeg
¼ teaspoon ground cinnamon	¼ teaspoon ground cinnamon
1 large onion	1 large onion
4 tomatoes	4 tomatoes
100 g/4 oz Cheddar cheese	1 cup grated Cheddar cheese
25 g/1 oz parsley, finely chopped	½ cup chopped parsley

Cut the aubergines (egg plants) into 2.5 cm/1 inch cubes. Put them into a collander and sprinkle them with the salt. Leave them to drain for 20 minutes. Rinse them under cold water and dry them with kitchen paper.

Cut the courgettes (zucchini) into 2.5 cm/1 inch cubes. Beat together the oil, lemon juice, garlic, pepper, nutmeg and cinnamon. Mix in the aubergines and courgettes (egg plants and zucchini) and leave them for 20 minutes.

Cut the onion into 2.5 cm/1 inch squares. Finely chop the tomatoes and dice the cheese.

Heat the grill to high. Alternate pieces of aubergine and courgette (egg plant and zucchini) on four kebab skewers, putting a square of onion after each piece. Grill the kebabs for about 10 minutes, turning them several times, so the vegetables are cooked through.

Put the tomatoes, cheese and parsley into separate small bowls. Serve a kebab and a warm pitta to each person.

Spiced Chickpea Pittas

Preparation time: 10 minutes
Waiting time: nil
Cooking time: 30 minutes

METRIC/IMPERIAL	AMERICAN
100 g/4 oz chickpeas, soaked and cooked, cooking liquid reserved	1 cup cooked chickpeas, cooking liquid reserved
2 tablespoons oil	2 tablespoons oil
1 medium onion, finely chopped	1 medium onion, finely chopped
1 garlic clove, finely chopped	1 garlic clove, finely chopped
1 teaspoon cumin seeds	1 teaspoon cumin seeds
1 teaspoon ground coriander	1 teaspoon ground coriander
½ teaspoon ground tumeric	½ teaspoon ground tumeric
2 teaspoons paprika	2 teaspoons chilli powder
pinch chilli powder	⅜ cup cooking liquid
6 tablespoons cooking liquid	2 teaspoons tomato paste
2 teaspoons tomato paste	*for serving:*
for serving:	½ lb tomatoes chopped
225 g/8 oz tomatoes, chopped	1 sweet green pepper, cored, seeded and cut into strips
1 green pepper, cored, seeded and cut into strips	1 large onion, quartered and sliced
1 large onion, quartered and sliced	1 lemon cut into wedges
1 lemon cut into wedges	

Heat the oil in a saucepan on a low heat. Mix in the onions, garlic and spices and cook until the onions are soft. Stir in the tomato paste and chickpeas. Pour in the cooking liquid and bring it to the boil. Cover and simmer gently for 30 minutes.

Fill warm pittas with the mixture. Serve the tomatoes, pepper, onion and lemon wedges in separate bowls.

Red Bean & Cheese Pittas

Preparation time: 15 minutes
Waiting time: nil
Cooking time: nil

METRIC/IMPERIAL	AMERICAN
100 g/4 oz red kidney beans, soaked and cooked	1 cup cooked red kidney beans
75 g/3 oz Edam cheese	3 oz Edam cheese
225 g/8 oz tomatoes	½ lb tomatoes
¼ cucumber	¼ cucumber
1 small onion	1 small onion
4 tablespoons chopped parsley	¼ cup chopped parsley
4 tablespoons olive oil	¼ cup olive oil
2 tablespoons red wine vinegar	2 tablespoons red wine vinegar
1 garlic clove, crushed with a pinch of sea salt	1 garlic clove, crushed with a pinch sea salt
1 tablespoon tomato paste	1 tablespoon tomato paste
1 teaspoon paprika	1 teaspoon paprika
freshly ground black pepper	freshly ground black pepper

Put the kidney beans into a bowl. Finely dice the cheese, tomatoes and cucumber. Quarter and thinly slice the onion. Add all these to the beans, together with the parsley.

Beat the remaining ingredients together to make the dressing. Fold it into the salad.

If wished, the tomatoes and cucumber may be served separately.

Tuna & Lemon Pittas

Preparation time: 15 minutes
Waiting time: nil
Cooking time: nil

METRIC/IMPERIAL	AMERICAN
one 200 g/7 oz tin tuna fish	one 200 g/ 7 oz tin tuna fish
4 oz flageolets or haricot beans, soaked and cooked	1 cup cooked haricot beans
12 black olives, halved and stoned	12 black olives, halved and stoned
1 small onion, finely chopped	1 small onion, finely chopped
4 tablespoons chopped parsley	¼ cup chopped parsley
1 lemon	1 lemon
4 tablespoons olive oil	¼ cup olive oil
freshly ground black pepper	freshly ground black pepper
4 small tomatoes	4 small tomatoes

Drain and flake the tuna. Mix it with the beans, olives, onion and parsley.

Cut the lemon in half. Cut the rind and pith from one half. Remove the seeds and finely chop the flesh. Mix the flesh into the tuna.

Squeeze the juice from the remaining lemon half and beat 1 tablespoon with the olive oil. Mix the resulting dressing into the tuna.

Chop the tomatoes and mix them into the rest just before filling and serving.

Curried Lentil Pittas

Preparation time: 15 minutes
Waiting time: nil
Cooking time: 1 hour

METRIC/IMPERIAL	AMERICAN
225 g/ 8 oz green lentils	1 cup green lentils
4 tablespoons oil	4 tablespoons oil
1 garlic clove, finely chopped	1 garlic clove, finely chopped
2 teaspoons hot Madras curry powder	2 teaspoons hot madras curry powder
1 teaspoon ground cumin	1 teaspoon ground cumin
575 ml/1 pint stock	2½ cups stock
1 bayleaf	1 bayleaf
1 small green pepper	1 small sweet green pepper
1 small red pepper	1 small sweet red pepper
1 small onion	1 small onion
2 tablespoons mango chutney	2 tablespoons mango chutney
juice ½ lemon	juice ½ lemon

Heat the oil in a saucepan on a low heat. Put in the garlic, curry powder and cumin. Stir until the garlic begins to sizzle. Stir in the lentils. Pour in the stock and bring it to the boil. Add the bayleaf. Cover and simmer until the lentils are tender and all the stock has been absorbed — 1 hour. Cool them and remove the bayleaf.

Cut the peppers into small, thin strips. Quarter and thinly slice the onion. Mix the mango chutney and lemon juice and then the peppers and onion into the lentils.

Avocado Salad Pittas

Preparation time: 20 minutes
Waiting time: nil
Cooking time: nil

METRIC/IMPERIAL	AMERICAN
1 ripe avocado	1 ripe avocado
40 g/1½ shelled walnuts	⅓ cup shelled walnut meats
100 g/4 oz tomatoes	¼ lb tomatoes
4 spring onions	4 spring onions
25 g/1 oz stoned dates	1 oz stoned dates
2 tablespoons natural yoghurt	2 tablespoons natural yoghurt
juice ½ lemon	juice ½ lemon
1 garlic clove, crushed with a pinch of sea salt	1 garlic clove, crushed with a pinch of sea salt
freshly ground black pepper	freshly ground black pepper
3 tablespoons chopped parsley	3 tablespoons chopped parsley

Halve, peel and stone the avocado. Finely chop half. Finely chop the walnuts. Chop the tomatoes, onions and dates.

Mash the remaining avocado half and mix in the yoghurt, lemon juice, garlic and pepper. Mix in all the remaining ingredients. Fill the pittas which may be warm or cold.

Centre: Cheese, Onion & Tomato Topping p. 80.
Clockwise from top left:
Mushroom & Ham Main Meal Topping p. 86.
Egg & Cheese Main Meal Topping p. 85.
Bacon & Apple Potato Topping p. 82.
Anchovy & Parsley Potato Topping p. 81.

Opposite page 77:
Top to bottom:
Nutty Salad Platter p. 105.
Watercress & Blue Cheese Salad p. 96.
Orange Salad p. 102.

Kabanos Pittas

Preparation time: 15 minutes
Waiting time: nil
Cooking time: nil

METRIC/IMPERIAL	AMERICAN
100 g/4 oz Polish Kabanos sausage	¼ lb Polish Kabanos sausage
1 red pepper	1 sweet red pepper
4 tomatoes	4 tomatoes
4 tablespoons chopped parsley	¼ cup chopped parsley
4 tablespoons oil	¼ cup oil
2 tablespoons white wine vinegar	2 tablespoons white wine vinegar
1 tablespoon tomato paste	1 tablespoon tomato paste
1 teaspoon paprika	1 teaspoon paprika
pinch cayenne pepper	pinch cayenne pepper
1 garlic clove, crushed with a pinch sea salt	1 garlic clove, crushed with a pinch sea salt
1 large onion, finely chopped	1 large onion, finely chopped

Thinly slice the sausage. Core, seed and chop the pepper. Chop the tomatoes. Mix the sausage, pepper and tomatoes with the parsley. Beat together the oil, vinegar, tomato paste, paprika, cayenne pepper and garlic. Mix them into the sausage.

Fill four pittas with the mixture. Serve the onion separately.

Melted Cheese & Prawn (Shrimp) Pittas

Preparation time: 15 minutes
Waiting time: nil
Cooking time: nil

METRIC/IMPERIAL	AMERICAN
175 g/6 oz Mozarella cheese	6 oz Mozarella cheese
175 g/6 oz peeled prawns	6 oz peeled shrimp
4 tomatoes, chopped	4 tomatoes, chopped
2 large pickled dill cucumbers, finely chopped	2 large pickled dill cucumbers, finely chopped
pinch cayenne pepper	pinch cayenne pepper

Heat the oven to 200C/400F/gas 6. Cut the cheese into small, thin squares. Put into a bowl with the remaining ingredients and toss to mix.

Slit the pittas and fill them with the cheese and prawn mixture. Lay them on a large, heatproof plate. Put them into the oven for 5 minutes so the cheese begins to melt.

Melted Cheese & Salami Pittas

Preparation time: 15 minutes
Waiting time: nil
Cooking time: 5 minutes

METRIC/IMPERIAL	AMERICAN
175 g/6 oz Bel Paese cheese	6 oz Bel Paese cheese
100 g/4 oz Italian salami, thinly sliced	¼ lb Italian salami, thinly sliced
16 black olives	16 black olives
4 tomatoes	4 tomatoes
1 garlic clove, finely chopped	1 garlic clove, finely chopped
4 tablespoons chopped parsley	¼ cup chopped parsley

Heat the oven to 200C/400F/gas 6. Cut the cheese into small thin slices. Cut the salami slices into quarters. Stone and quarter the olives. Chop the tomatoes. Mix these together, adding the garlic and parsley.

Slit the pittas and fill them with the mixture. Lay them on a large heatproof plate. Put them into the oven for 5 minutes so the cheese begins to melt.

POTATO BAKE

How can you get the best from a potato? The answer is to bake it in its jacket. This preserves both flavour and goodness without adding extra fat to the meal.

A jacket potato makes a suitable and satisfying accompaniment to burgers, grills and salads. Serve it plainly or topped with a little butter, soured cream or natural yoghurt; or with one of a variety of colourful toppings.

If you make the topping more substantial, a jacket potato can be a meal in itself. All you will need to accompany it is a mixed salad. Choose even shaped, unblemished potatoes for baking. As an accompaniment, each one should weigh about 175 g/6 oz. For a main meal, choose them slightly larger, about 225 g/8 oz.

Baking potatoes in their jackets is one of the easiest of cooking processes. Scrub the potatoes under cold running water and then prick them twice on both sides with a fork. Place them on the oven rack, turn the oven to 200C/400F/gas 6 and leave the potatoes for 1 hour 30 minutes. If the oven is already up to temperature, the potatoes will only need to cook for 1 hour 15 minutes. When they are done, they should have crisp skins and soft middles.

In some restaurants, the cooked potatoes are stood on one end, a cross cut is made in the top and a small piece of butter put inside. This is fine if you only have a small amount of topping. Where larger amounts are involved such as in the recipes below, it is best to cut the potato lengthways in half so that you have two fairly flat pieces. Cut several scores in the flesh of each one and put on the topping while the potatoes are still hot. Be a little careful when choosing the topping and make sure that the flavour goes with that of the main dish.

When eating a jacket potato, don't forget to eat the skin! Pick it up with your fingers and eat it like a biscuit if you like! It tastes good and contains both vitamins and fibre.

Cheese, Onion & Tomato Potato Topping

Preparation time: 15 minutes
Waiting time: nil
Cooking time: nil

METRIC/IMPERIAL
75 g/3 oz Cheddar cheese, finely grated
½ teaspoon mustard powder
1 tablespoon tomato paste
2 spring onions
2 small tomatoes

AMERICAN
¾ cup finely grated Cheddar cheese
½ teaspoon mustard powder
1 tablespoon tomato paste
2 spring onions
2 small tomatoes

Put the cheese into a bowl and mix in the mustard powder and tomato paste. Finely chop the onions and tomatoes and mix them into the cheese.

Anchovy and Parsley Potato Topping

Preparation time: 15 minutes
Waiting time: nil
Cooking time: nil

METRIC/IMPERIAL	AMERICAN
8 anchovy fillets	8 anchovy fillets
4 tablespoons olive oil	¼ cup olive oil
juice 1 lemon	juice 1 lemon
freshly ground black pepper	freshly ground black pepper
6 tablespoons chopped parsley	⅜ cup chopped parsley

Finely chop the anchovy fillets and, using a pestle and mortar, pound them to a paste. Gradually work in first the oil and then the lemon juice. Season with plenty of pepper and mix in the parsley.

This makes a fairly small amount of topping, but it has a strong flavour and so a little goes a long way.

Avocado Potato Topping

Preparation time: 15 minutes
Waiting time: nil
Cooking time: nil

METRIC/IMPERIAL	AMERICAN
2 ripe avocados	2 ripe avocados
2 tablespoons tahini (sesame paste)	2 tablespoons tahini (sesame paste)
2 teaspoons tomato paste	2 teaspoons tomato paste
2 tablespoons chopped chives	2 tablespoons chopped chives
¼ teaspoon Tabasco sauce	¼ teaspoon Tabasco sauce

Peel, stone and mash the avocados. Beat in the remaining ingredients. Halve the potatoes and pile the mixture on top.

Bacon & Apple Potato Topping

Preparation time: 5 minutes
Waiting time: nil
Cooking time: 10 minutes

METRIC/IMPERIAL	AMERICAN
75 g/3 oz lean back bacon	3 oz lean back bacon
1 medium cooking apple	1 medium cooking apple
1 medium onion	1 medium onion
25 g/1 oz butter	2 tablespoons butter
4 sage leaves, chopped	4 sage leaves, chopped
½ teaspoon mustard powder	½ teaspoon mustard powder

Finely chop the bacon. Peel, core and finely chop the apple. Finely chop the onion.

Melt the butter in a frying pan on a low heat. Put in the bacon, apple, onion, sage and mustard powder. Cover the pan and cook them gently for 10 minutes so the apple and onion are soft and the bacon cooked through.

Curried Peanut Potato Topping

Preparation time: 10 minutes
Waiting time: nil
Cooking time: nil

METRIC/IMPERIAL	AMERICAN
3 tablespoons crunchy peanut butter	3 tablespoons crunchy peanut butter
6 tablespoons natural yoghurt	⅜ cup natural yoghurt
¼ teaspoon curry paste	¼ teaspoon curry paste
8 small parsley sprigs	8 small parsley sprigs

Put the peanut butter into a bowl and gradually beat in the yoghurt. Add the curry paste and mix well.

Spoon the topping over the potato halves and top each half with a parsley sprig.

Jacket Potato with Cheese & Sausages

Preparation time: 15 minutes
Waiting time: nil
Cooking time: 25 minutes

METRIC/IMPERIAL	AMERICAN
175 g/6 oz Cheddar cheese, grated	¾ cup grated Cheddar cheese
4 tablespoons sweet chutney	¼ cup sweet chutney
8 good quality pork sausages	8 good quality pork sausages

Mix the cheese with the chutney. Put the sausages on a rack in a roasting tin. Put them into the oven with the potatoes for 25 minutes or until cooked through.

Halve each potato and top each half with cheese. Make a slit through the cheese and the potato and push in a sausage.

Spanish Potato Topping

Preparation time: 5 minutes
Waiting time: nil
Cooking time: 10 minutes

METRIC/IMPERIAL	AMERICAN
175 g/6 oz Spanish chorizo sausage	6 oz Spanish chorizo sausage
2 green peppers	2 sweet green peppers
125 g/4 fl oz tomato juice	½ cup tomato juice

Finely chop the chorizo. Core, seed and finely chop the peppers.

Put the chorizo into a frying pan without any fat. Set it on a low heat until it's own fat begins to melt. Put in the peppers and cook them, stirring occasionally, until they are soft.

Pour in the tomato juice and bring it to the boil. Simmer for 1 minute before spooning the topping over the potatoes.

Creamy Pepper Potato Topping

Preparation time: 20 minutes
Waiting time: nil
Cooking time: nil

METRIC/IMPERIAL	AMERICAN
100 g/4 oz fromage blanc or other smooth, low fat soft cheese	¼ lb fromage blanc or other smooth, low fat soft cheese
2 tablespoons mayonnaise	2 tablespoons mayonnaise
2 tablespoons soured cream	2 tablespoons soured cream
1 small red pepper	1 small sweet red pepper
1 small green pepper	1 small sweet green pepper
2 tablespoons chopped parsley	2 tablespoons chopped parsley
1 garlic clove, crushed with a pinch of sea salt	1 garlic clove, crushed with a pinch of sea salt
1 teaspoon paprika	1 teaspoon paprika

Cream the cheese in a bowl. Beat in the mayonnaise and soured cream. Core and seed the peppers and cut them into 2.5 cm/1 inch squares. Grate the pepper flesh into the cheese mixture, leaving the skin behind. Beat in the parsley, garlic and paprika.

Redcurrant Potato Topping

Preparation time: 15 minutes
Waiting time: nil
Cooking time: nil

METRIC/IMPERIAL	AMERICAN
175 g/6 oz curd (or other low fat soft) cheese	¾ cup curd (or other low fat soft) cheese
1 tablespoon redcurrant jelly	1 tablespoon redcurrant jelly
2 teaspoons Dijon mustard	2 teaspoon Dijon mustard
2 tablespoons chopped mint	2 tablespoons chopped mint
2 tablespoons chopped chives	2 tablespoons chopped chives

Put the cheese into a bowl. Melt, and then cool, the redcurrant jelly. Beat it into the cheese. Beat in the mustard and herbs.

Egg & Cheese Main Meal Topping

Preparation time: 15 minutes
Waiting time: nil
Cooking time: nil

METRIC/IMPERIAL	AMERICAN
4 eggs, hard boiled	4 hard cooked eggs
225 g/8 oz cottage cheese	1 cup cottage cheese
3 tablespoons mayonnaise	3 tablespoons mayonnaise
4 tablespoons chopped chives	¼ cup chopped chives
4 tablespoons chopped parsley	¼ cup chopped parsley
pinch cayenne pepper	pinch cayenne pepper
8 small parsley sprigs	8 small parsley sprigs

Mash the eggs and mix them with the cheese, chopped herbs and cayenne pepper.

Pile the mixture onto the potato halves and top each half with a parsley sprig.

Mushroom & Ham Main Meal Topping

Preparation time: 10 minutes
Waiting time: nil
Cooking time: 10 minutes

METRIC/IMPERIAL	AMERICAN
350 g/12 oz flat mushrooms	¾ lb flat mushrooms
350–450 g/12 oz–1 lb cooked lean ham	¾–1 lb cooked lean ham
25 g/1 oz butter	2 tablespoons butter
1 large onion, finely chopped	1 large onion, finely chopped
2 tablespoons chopped thyme	2 tablespoons chopped thyme
4 sage leaves, chopped	4 sage leaves, chopped
4 tablespoons soured cream	¼ cup soured cream

Finely chop the mushrooms and the ham. Melt the butter in a frying pan on a low heat. Put in the onion and soften it. Raise the heat, stir in the mushrooms, ham and herbs and cook them, stirring, for 1 minute. This quick, high cooking should keep the mixture fairly dry.

Stir in the soured cream. Let it just heat through and serve immediately.

Black Bean Main Meal Topping

Preparation time: 15 minutes
Waiting time: nil
Cooking time: 15 minutes

METRIC/IMPERIAL	AMERICAN
175 g/6 oz black kidney beans, soaked and cooked	1 cup black kidney beans, soaked and cooked
225 g/8 oz tomatoes	½ lb tomatoes
3 tablespoons oil	3 tablespoons oil
1 large onion, quartered and thinly sliced	1 large onion, quartered and thinly sliced
1 garlic clove, finely chopped	1 garlic clove, finely chopped
1 teaspoon paprika	1 teaspoon paprika
¼ teaspoon Tabasco sauce	¼ teaspoon Tabasco sauce
1 tablespoon white wine vinegar	1 tablespoon white wine vinegar
4 tablespoons natural yoghurt	¼ cup natural yoghurt
4 tablespoons chopped parsley	¼ cup chopped parsley

Scald, skin and chop the tomatoes. Heat the oil in a saucepan on a low heat. Put in the onion and garlic and soften them. Add the tomatoes, paprika, Tabasco sauce and vinegar and stir in the beans. Simmer, uncovered, for 15 minutes or until the mixture is fairly dry. Take the pan from the heat and wait until the contents come off the boil. Stir in the yoghurt and parsley.

Curried Vegetable Main Meal Topping

Preparation time: 30 minutes
Waiting time: nil
Cooking time: 30 minutes

METRIC/IMPERIAL	AMERICAN
275 ml/½ pint natural yoghurt	1¼ cups natural yoghurt
½ tablespoon cornflour	½ tablespoon cornflour
350 g/12 oz aubergines	¾ lb egg plant
1 tablespoon sea salt	1 tablespoon sea salt
225 g/8 oz carrots	½ lb carrots
1 small cauliflower	1 small cauliflower
1 large green pepper	1 large sweet green pepper
1 large onion	1 large onion
3 tablespoons oil	3 tablespoons oil
1 garlic clove, finely chopped	1 garlic clove, finely chopped
2 teaspoons curry powder	2 teaspoons curry powder
50 g/2 oz cashew nut pieces	⅝ cup cashew nut pieces
40 g/1½ oz creamed coconut	1½ oz creamed coconut

Put the cornflour into a saucepan and stir in the yoghurt. Set them on a medium heat and bring them to the boil, stirring. Stir for 5 minutes or until the mixture is smooth and thick. Take the pan from the heat.

Finely dice the aubergines (egg plants). Put them into a collander and sprinkle them with the salt. Leave them to drain for 15 minutes. Rinse them with cold water and dry them with kitchen paper.

Finely chop the carrots and cauliflower. Core, seed and finely chop the pepper. Finely chop the onion.

Heat the oil in a saucepan on a low heat. Put in the onion and garlic and soften them. Put in the cashew nuts, peppers and curry powder and cook, stirring frequently, until the onions and cashew nuts are golden. Stir in the aubergines (egg plants), carrot and cauliflower.

Pour in the yoghurt and bring it to the boil. Add the creamed coconut, in small pieces. Lower the heat and simmer gently for 30 minutes, stirring several times. The vegetables should be just tender.

Beef & Vegetable Main Meal Topping

Preparation time: 15 minutes
Waiting time: nil
Cooking time: 45 minutes

METRIC/IMPERIAL	AMERICAN
450 g/1 lb minced beef	1 lb ground beef
4 celery sticks	4 celery sticks
225 g/8 oz carrots	½ lb carrots
1 large onion	1 large onion
1 small cooking apple	1 small cooking apple
4 tablespoons oil	¼ cup oil
1 garlic clove, finely chopped	1 garlic clove, finely chopped
125 ml/4 fl oz tomato juice	½ cup tomato juice
2 teaspoons dried mixed herbs	2 teaspoons dried mixed herbs
25 g/1 oz Parmesan cheese, grated	2 tablespoons grated Parmesan cheese

Finely chop the celery, carrots and onion. Peel, core and finely grate the apple.

Heat the oil in a saucepan on a low heat. Mix in the celery, carrots, onion and garlic and cook them, stirring occasionally until they are just beginning to brown. Mix in the beef and stir until it browns.

Pour in the tomato juice and bring it to the boil. Add the apple and herbs. Cover and simmer for 45 minutes.

Spoon the beef mixture over the potato halves and scatter the Parmesan cheese over the top.

Smoked Fish Main Meal Topping

Preparation time: 20 minutes
Waiting time: nil
Cooking time: 4 minutes

METRIC/IMPERIAL	AMERICAN
450 g/1 lb smoked haddock fillets	1 lb smoked haddock fillets
150 ml/¼ pint milk	⅝ cup milk
150 ml/¼ pint water	⅝ cup water
1 parsley sprig	1 parsley sprig
1 teaspoon black peppercorns	1 teaspoon black peppercorns
25 g/1 oz butter	2 tablespoons butter
1 large onion, thinly sliced	1 large onion, thinly sliced
3 tablespoons wholewheat flour	3 tablespoons wholewheat flour
freshly ground black pepper	freshly ground black pepper
4 tablespoons chopped parsley	¼ cup chopped parsley
1 tablespoon chopped capers	1 tablespoon chopped capers

Put the fish into a shallow pan with the milk, water, parsley sprig and peppercorns. Bring it to the boil, simmer it for 2 minutes and take it from the heat. Lift out the fish. Skin, bone and flake it. Strain and reserve the cooking liquid.

Melt the butter in a saucepan on a low heat. Stir in the flour and the reserved liquid. Bring them to the boil, stirring, and simmer for 2 minutes. Season with the pepper. Take the pan from the heat and stir in the parsley, capers and fish.

CHEF'S SPECIAL SALADS

Fresh mixed salads are a natural accompaniment to all fast food meals. They can be quickly prepared without fuss and will not deteriorate if they have to be kept waiting. They are easy to eat and their freshness goes so well with the various grilled foods, pizzas, pittas and potatoes. A salad can always be made to look so much more attractive than cooked vegetables. You can also vary both basic ingredients and dressings to add variety.

When you are preparing a side salad, make sure that all the ingredients go together well, both in flavour and texture. Something soft, such as tomatoes, for example, will not make a very good companion for something hard and crunchy like white cabbage.

Always choose salad ingredients that will match well with the main dish. This also applies to the dressing. Think about the flavours and make sure that they will not clash or that they are not providing something too similar. For example, a salad with a cheese dressing, plus burgers or a grill topped with cheese will be too much of a good thing.

Don't just randomly slap salad ingredients onto a plate. Arrange them attractively, matching colours and shapes. This adds tremendously to the salad's appeal and ensures that this side dish, full of fresh goodness, will be eaten up and enjoyed.

The Chef's Special Salad, usually containing a mixture of cheese and cold meats, can be found on many fast food menus. You can make all kinds of Chef's Specials, using different meats, fish, eggs, cheese, nuts and beans. Think of all the vegetable ingredients that you can add to them and you have an amazing selection of combinations to choose from. All you have to do is make sure that flavours and textures go well together; that the dressing complements them; and that they are attractively arranged.

Basic Vinaigrette Dressing

Preparation time: 5 minutes
Waiting time: nil
Cooking time: nil

METRIC/IMPERIAL	AMERICAN
4 tablespoons oil	¼ cup oil
2 tablespoons white wine vinegar	2 tablespoons white wine vinegar
1 garlic clove, crushed with a pinch sea salt	1 garlic clove crushed with pinch sea salt
freshly ground black pepper	freshly ground black pepper

Beat all the ingredients together well.

Variations

Oils to use: Olive, sunflower, safflower, groundnut, corn, sesame. Use virgin oil or cold pressed nut and seed oils whenever possible for goodness and flavour.

Vinegars: Instead of white wine vinegar use a red wine or cider vinegar or the juice of ½ lemon or lime. If the flavour of orange is required, add 2 tablespoons freshly squeezed orange juice to the basic vinaigrette as it is not sharp enough to be used alone.

Garlic: Garlic can be replaced with chopped chives or a little grated onion.

Seasonings: These can be varied. Salt can be omitted; black pepper can be replaced with white, or a pinch of cayenne, chilli powder, or ¼ teaspoon Tabasco sauce. Paprika (½-1 teaspoon) can be added with these. ½ teaspoon mustard powder, ¼ teaspoon English mustard or 1 teaspoon mild mustard can be added instead of the pepper.

Top to bottom:
Mixed Bean Salad p. 100.
Cooked Vegetable & Soured Cream Salad p. 98.
Chicken, Bean & Sesame Salad p. 99.

Opposite page 93:
Clockwise from top left:
Sweet & Sour Cucumber Relish p. 115.
Mushroom Relish p. 119.
Uncooked Cranberry Relish p. 118.
Corn & Chilli Relish p. 113.
Tomato, Celery & Red Pepper Relish p. 110.
Horseradish & Orange Relish p. 117.

Other flavourings: 1 tablespoon tomato paste; 1 tablespoon Worcestershire sauce; 1 tablespoon tamari, shoyu or soy sauce; ¼ teaspoon curry paste.

Herbs: A selection of chopped fresh herbs can be added to the dressing. If you are using dried herbs let them soak in the dressing for at least 30 minutes before dressing the salad.

Walnut dressing

Using a pestle and mortar, pound 2 tablespoons chopped shelled walnuts to a paste. Work in the basic vinaigrette dressing plus one tablespoon each chopped basil and parsley.

Prawn (shrimp) Dressing

Using a pestle and mortar pound 2 tablespoons chopped prawns (shrimps) to a paste. Work in 1 tablespoon tomato paste, ½ teaspoon paprika, a pinch cayenne pepper and the basic dressing.

Basic Mayonnaise

Preparation time: 20 minutes

METRIC/IMPERIAL	AMERICAN
2 egg yolks	2 egg yolks
1 teaspoon mustard powder	1 teaspoon mustard powder
freshly ground black pepper	freshly ground black pepper
225 ml/8 fl oz oil	1 cup oil
3 tablespoons white wine vinegar	3 tablespoons white wine vinegar

Beat the egg yolks together in a bowl. Add the mustard powder and pepper and beat again. Add 2 tablespoons of the oil, drop by drop, beating well after each addition. Beat in 2 teaspoons vinegar and then the rest of the oil by the teaspoon at first and then by the tablespoon. Add the remaining vinegar by the teaspoon to taste.

Oils: Do not use too strong an oil for mayonnaise. Use a mild flavoured olive oil or a refined nut or seed oil. Cold pressed oils have too strong a flavour.

Flavourings: Add a crushed garlic clove when beating the egg yolks for the first time. The mustard powder can be replaced with a teaspoon of mild mustard or ¼ teaspoon curry paste.

Add 1 tablespoon tomato paste with the first vinegar.

Add any selection of chopped fresh herbs. Dried herbs are not suitable.

Yoghurt Dressings

Preparation time: 5-20 minutes
Waiting time: nil
Cooking time: nil

Garlic, seasoning, herbs and other flavourings can all be beaten into natural yoghurt to make a salad dressing. Yoghurt alone can be used successfully. You can also beat in 1 tablespoon oil to every 4 tablespoons (¼ cup) yoghurt. A little lemon juice can also be added if the yoghurt is a particularly sweet one.

Yoghurt & Mayonnaise Dressing

Mix equal portions of natural yoghurt and mayonnaise.

Yoghurt Mayonnaise

Beat 2 egg yolks in a bowl. Gradually beat in 4 tablespoons oil, taking care not to let the mixture curdle. Beat in 150 ml/¼ pint/⅝ cup yoghurt, one teaspoon at a time for the first 6 teaspoons, then 1 tablespoon at a time. Add 1 teaspoon mustard powder or Dijon mustard and freshly ground black pepper.

Yoghurt & Curd Cheese Dressing

Put 100 g/4 oz/½ cup curd cheese into a bowl and gradually beat in 3 tablespoons yoghurt and ½ teaspoon Dijon mustard. Mix in 2 tablespoons chopped parsley.

Yoghurt & Blue Cheese Dressing

Grate or crumble 40 g/1½ oz blue cheese, depending on the texture. Gradually work in 6 tablespoons yoghurt. Beat in 1 clove garlic, crushed with a pinch of sea salt, and a pinch of cayenne pepper.

Tahini Dressing

Preparation time: 10 minutes
Waiting time: nil
Cooking time: nil

METRIC/IMPERIAL	AMERICAN
1 tablespoon tahini (sesame paste)	1 tablespoon tahini (sesame paste)
4 tablespoons sesame or sunflower oil	4 tablespoons sesame or sunflower oil
1 tablespoon tamari, soy or shoyu sauce	1 tablespoon tamari, soy or shoyu sauce
2 tablespoons cider vinegar	2 tablespoons cider vinegar
1 garlic clove, crushed with a pinch sea salt	1 garlic clove, crushed with a pinch sea salt
freshly ground black pepper	freshly ground black pepper

Put the tahini into a bowl and gradually beat in the oil. Add the remaining ingredients and beat well.

Cucumber Pickle Salad

Preparation time: 20 minutes
Waiting time: nil
Cooking time: nil

METRIC/IMPERIAL	AMERICAN
1 large cucumber	1 large cucumber
2 red peppers	2 sweet red peppers
1 cos lettuce	1 cos lettuce
6 tablespoons natural yoghurt	⅜ cup natural yoghurt
100 g/4 oz quark or other low fat soft cheese	½ cup quark or other low fat soft cheese
1 tablespoon chopped tarragon	1 tablespoon chopped tarragon
1 tablespoon chopped mint	1 tablespoon chopped mint
2 pickled dill cucumbers	2 pickled dill cucumbers

Thinly slice the cucumber. Core and seed the peppers and cut them into 2.5 cm/1 inch strips. Arrange a bed of lettuce on each of 4 small plates and arrange an overlapping spiral of cucumber slices in the centre.

Beat together the yoghurt, cheese and herbs. Finely chop the dill cucumbers and mix them in. Pile the mixture on top of the cucumbers. Surround the cucumbers with pieces of red pepper.

Watercress & Blue Cheese Salad

Preparation time: 20 minutes
Waiting time: nil
Cooking time: nil

METRIC/IMPERIAL	AMERICAN
175 g/6 oz watercress	6 oz watercress
4 tomatoes	4 tomatoes
16 radishes	16 radishes
50 g/2 oz shelled walnuts	¼ cup walnut meats
50 g/ 2 oz blue cheese	2 oz blue cheese
pinch cayenne pepper	pinch cayenne pepper
4 tablespoons oil	¼ cup oil
2 tablespoons white wine vinegar	2 tablespoons white wine vinegar
1 garlic clove, crushed	1 garlic clove, crushed
4 small parsley sprigs	4 small parsley sprigs

Chop the watercress and divide it between 4 small plates. Cut each tomato into four slices. Arrange them in the centre of the watercress. Thinly slice the radishes and finely chop the walnuts. Scatter them around the tomatoes.

Grate or cream the cheese, depending on the texture. Beat in the cayenne pepper, oil, vinegar and garlic. Spoon the resulting dressing over the tomatoes and top it with a parsley sprig.

Crunchy Salad

Preparation time: 20 minutes
Waiting time: nil
Cooking time: nil

METRIC/IMPERIAL	AMERICAN
225 g/8 oz white cabbage	½ lb white cabbage
175 g/6 oz carrots	6 oz carrots
50 g/2 oz white grapes	2 oz white grapes
4 tablespoons oil	¼ cup oil
2 tablespoons white wine vinegar	2 tablespoons white wine vinegar
1 garlic clove, crushed with a pinch of sea salt	1 garlic clove, crushed with a pinch sea salt
freshly ground black pepper	freshly ground black pepper
4 large celery sticks	4 large celery sticks
4 tablespoons soured cream	¼ cup soured cream
juice ½ lemon	juice ½ lemon
1 teaspoon honey	1 teaspoon honey
¼ teaspoon mustard powder	¼ teaspoon mustard powder
50 g/2 oz shelled almonds	⅓ cup almond nut meats
25 g/1 oz shelled peanuts	2 tablespoons peanuts

Shred the cabbage, finely grate the carrots and halve and seed the grapes. Put them into a bowl. Beat together the oil, vinegar, garlic and pepper and fold them into the cabbage mixture.

Finely chop the celery. Mix together the soured cream, lemon juice, honey and mustard powder. Fold in the celery and all but four of the almonds.

Put a portion of the celery salad in the centre of each of four plates. Top it with an almond. Surround it with the cabbage salad. Scatter the peanuts over the cabbage salad.

Cooked Vegetable & Soured Cream Salad

Preparation time: 20 minutes
Waiting time: nil
Cooking time: 20 minutes

METRIC/IMPERIAL	AMERICAN
275 ml/½ pint soured cream	1¼ cups soured cream
1 tablespoon grated horseradish	1 tablespoon grated horseradish
1 tablespoon red wine vinegar	1 tablespoon red wine vinegar
2 teaspoons Dijon mustard	2 teaspoons Dijon mustard
2 tablespoons chopped chives	2 tablespoons chopped chives
1 teaspoon honey	1 teaspoon honey
1 tablespoon lemon juice	1 tablespoon lemon juice
1 tablespoon chopped mint	1 tablespoon chopped mint
350 g/12 oz beetroot	¾ lb beetroot
450 g/1 lb potatoes	1 lb potatoes
225 g/8 oz shelled peas	½ lb shelled peas
225 g/8 oz carrots, finely diced	½ lb carrots, finely diced
1 lettuce	1 lettuce
8 small parsley sprigs	8 small parsley sprigs

Divide the soured cream into three portions. Into one, mix the horseradish and red wine vinegar; into the second, the Dijon mustard and chives; and into the third the honey, lemon juice and mint.

Cook the beetroot until tender. Skin and dice it amd mix it into the horseradish dressing. Boil or steam the potatoes in their skins. Skin and dice them and mix them into the mustard dressing.

Steam the peas and the carrots together. Mix them into the honey dressing.

Arrange a bed of lettuce on each of four plates. Put in a portion of the beetroot and a portion of the potatoes, close together in the centre. Scatter the pea and carrot salad round the edge. Top the beetroot and the potato salads with a parsley sprig.

Chicken, Bean & Sesame Salad

Preparation time: 40 minutes
Waiting time: nil
Cooking time: nil

METRIC/IMPERIAL	AMERICAN
one 1.125 kg/2½ lb chicken roasted	one 2½ lb chicken, roasted
225 g/8 oz shelled broad beans, or	½ lb shelled broad beans or
100 g/4 oz haricot beans, soaked and	1 cup cooked haricot beans
cooked	¼ cup oil
4 tablespoons oil	juice ½ lemon
juice ½ lemon	2 tablespoons chopped parsley
2 tablespoons chopped parsley	freshly ground black pepper
freshly ground black pepper	¼ cup mayonnaise
4 tablespoons mayonnaise	¼ cup natural yoghurt
4 tablespoons natural yoghurt	1 tablespoon tahini (sesame paste)
1 tablespoon tahini (sesame paste)	pinch chilli powder
pinch chilli powder	1 cos lettuce
1 cos lettuce	4 tomatoes
4 tomatoes	16 slices cucumber
16 slices cucumber	2 tablespoons sesame seeds
2 tablespoon sesame seeds	8 black olives
8 black olives	

Cut the chicken meat from the bones and dice it. Steam the broad beans for 20 minutes or until tender.

Beat together the oil, lemon juice, parsley and pepper. Mix in the beans. Beat together the mayonnaise, yoghurt, tahini and chilli powder.

Arrange a bed of lettuce on each of four plates. Put a portion of the chicken in the centre and spoon the tahini dressing over the top. Put a portion of the beans on either side.

Quarter the tomatoes and put one quarter either side of each pile of beans. Put two cucumber slices between the tomato quarters.

Scatter the sesame seeds over the chicken. Halve and stone the olives. Put one olive half on top of each pile of beans and two on top of the chicken.

Mixed Bean Salad

Preparation time: 40 minutes
Waiting time: nil
Cooking time: nil

METRIC/IMPERIAL	AMERICAN
100 g/4 oz red kidney beans, soaked and cooked	1 cup cooked red kidney beans
100 g/4 oz flageolets or white kidney beans, soaked and cooked	1 cup cooked flageolets or white kidney beans
50 g/2 oz boiling sausage or other thin continental sausage	2 oz boiling sausage or other thin continental sausage
50 g/2 oz cooked lean ham	2 oz cooked lean ham
2 eggs, hard boiled	2 hard cooked eggs
4 spring onions, finely chopped	4 spring onions, finely chopped
4 tablespoons oil	¼ cup oil
1 tablespoon red wine vinegar	1 tablespoon red wine vinegar
½ tablespoon chopped thyme	½ tablespoon chopped thyme
½ garlic clove, crushed	½ garlic clove, crushed
1 teaspoon tomato paste	1 teaspoon tomato paste
¼ teaspoon Tabasco sauce	¼ teaspoon Tabasco sauce
1 tablespoon cider vinegar	1 tablespoon cider vinegar
2 tablespoons chopped parsley	2 tablespoons chopped parsley
½ teaspoon Dijon mustard	½ teaspoon Dijon mustard
1 lettuce	1 lettuce
½ cucumber, thinly sliced	½ cucumber, thinly sliced
4 tomatoes	4 tomatoes

Mix together the red kidney beans and sausage. Mix together the flageolets, ham, eggs and spring onions.

Beat together half the oil, the red wine vinegar, thyme, garlic, tomato paste and Tabasco sauce. Fold the mixture into the red beans. Beat together the remaining oil, the cider vinegar, parsley and mustard. Fold them into the flageolets.

Arrange a bed of lettuce on each of four small plates. Put a portion of the flageolet salad in the centre. Surround it with a portion of the red bean salad.

Garnish the salads with tomato wedges and cucumber slices.

Egg, Prawn & Crab Salad

Preparation time: 45 minutes
Waiting time: nil
Cooking time: nil

METRIC/IMPERIAL	AMERICAN
6 eggs, hard boiled	6 hard cooked eggs
1 teaspoon mustard powder	1 teaspoon mustard powder
225 ml/8 fl oz sunflower oil	1 cup sunflower oil
2 tablespoons white wine vinegar	2 tablespoons white wine vinegar
225 g/8 oz shelled prawns	2 cups shelled shrimp
½ teaspoon paprika	½ teaspoon paprika
cayenne pepper	cayenne pepper
1 pickled dill cucumber, finely chopped	1 pickled dill cucumber, finely chopped
½ large cucumber	½ large cucumber
1 red pepper	1 sweet red pepper
1 ripe avocado	1 ripe avocado
1 cos lettuce	1 cos lettuce
225 g/8 oz crab meat	1½ cups crabmeat
1 box mustard and cress	1 box mustard and cress

Take the yolks from two of the eggs. Sieve them into a bowl. Add the mustard powder. Drop by drop, beat in 2 tablespoons of the oil and then 1 tablespoon of the vinegar, 1 teaspoon at a time. Very carefully, slowly beat in the remaining oil so you have a thick mayonnaise-type sauce. Divide it into two.

Take 50 g/2 oz of the prawns (shrimp) and pound them to a paste with a pestle and mortar. Add them to one half of the mayonnaise, together with the paprika and a pinch of cayenne pepper. Mix the dill cucumber into the other half of the sauce.

Finely dice the half cucumber and core, seed and dice the pepper. Mix them together. Quarter, stone and peel the avocado. Cut each quarter in half lengthways and each piece again in half crossways.

Lay a bed of lettuce leaves on each of four plates. Put a portion of the mixed cucumber and pepper in the centre.

Halve the eggs. Put a half, cut side down, on either side of the salad. Put a portion of the remaining prawns (shrimp) on the third quarter of the plate and opposite it, a portion of the crab. Put a piece of avocado on each side of the prawns (shrimp) and the crab.

Spoon the prawn (shrimp) sauce over the eggs and the dill cucumber sauce over the prawns (shrimp) and the crab. Cut tufts of mustard and cress and put them on top of the cucumber and pepper. Sprinkle a very little cayenne pepper over the prawns (shrimp) and crab.

Orange Salad

Preparation time: 15 minutes
Waiting time: nil
Cooking time: nil

METRIC/IMPERIAL	AMERICAN
4 medium oranges	4 medium oranges
1 lettuce	1 lettuce
65 g/2½ oz watercress	2½ oz watercress
40 g/1½ oz currants	1½ oz currants
2 boxes mustard and cress	2 boxes mustard and cress
4 tablespoons olive oil	¼ cup olive oil
juice ½ lemon	juice ½ lemon
1 teaspoon Dijon mustard	1 teaspoon Dijon mustard
1 garlic clove, crushed with a pinch of sea salt	1 garlic clove, crushed with a pinch sea salt
2 white grapes	2 white grapes

Cut the peel and pith from the oranges. Cut the segments away from the skin and remove any pips. Arrange a bed of lettuce on each of four side plates. Chop the watercress and arrange it on top. Scatter on the currants. Put a ring of mustard and cress round the outside of each plate.

Beat together the oil, lemon juice, mustard and garlic and spoon the resulting dressing over the salad.

Arrange the orange segments in a star pattern on top. Halve and seed the grapes and put half in the centre of each orange star.

Cheese Salad Platter

Preparation time: 40 minutes
Waiting time: nil
Cooking time: nil

METRIC/IMPERIAL   AMERICAN

Tomato, cheese and onion salad

METRIC/IMPERIAL	AMERICAN
350 g/12 oz tomatoes	¾ lb tomatoes
3 tablespoons olive oil	3 tablespoons olive oil
1 large onion, thinly sliced	1 large onion, thinly sliced
1 garlic clove, finely chopped	1 garlic clove, finely chopped
1½ tablespoons white wine vinegar	1½ tablespoons white wine vinegar
2 tablespoons chopped parsley	2 tablespoons chopped parsley
1 tablespoon chopped basil (if available)	1 tablespoon chopped basil (if available)
freshly ground black pepper	freshly ground black pepper
50 g/2 oz Mozarella cheese	2 oz Mozarella cheese

Watercress, apple and cheese salad

METRIC/IMPERIAL	AMERICAN
75 g/3 oz watercress	3 oz watercress
1 dessert apple	1 dessert apple
½ small onion	½ small onion
2 tablespoons olive oil	2 tablespoons olive oil
1 tablespoon cider vinegar	1 tablespoon cider vinegar
sea salt and freshly ground black pepper	sea salt and freshly ground black pepper
40 g/1½ oz Cheddar cheese, finely grated	⅜ cup finely grated Cheddar cheese

Fennel, cheese and walnut salad

METRIC/IMPERIAL	AMERICAN
1 small bulb fennel	1 small bulb fennel
50 g/2 oz shelled walnuts, finely chopped	¼ cup walnut meats, finely chopped
50 g/2 oz soft blue cheese	2 oz soft blue cheese
6 tablespoons natural yoghurt	⅜ cup natural yoghurt
pinch cayenne pepper	pinch cayenne pepper
½ garlic clove, crushed	½ garlic clove, crushed

Celery and cucumber with cheese topping

175 g/6 oz curd cheese	¾ cup curd cheese
4 tablespoons chopped parsley	¼ cup chopped parsley
1 garlic clove, crushed with a pinch of sea salt	1 garlic clove, crushed with a pinch of sea salt
4 celery sticks	4 celery sticks
4 thick cucumber slices	4 thick cucumber slices
4 hazelnuts	4 hazelnuts
12 almonds	12 almonds

Tomato, cheese and onion salad

Cut the tomatoes into thin wedges. Heat the oil in a saucepan on a low heat. Put in the onion and garlic and soften them. Add the vinegar and take the pan from the heat. Cool the onions completely. Mix in the parsley, basil and pepper. Cut the cheese into small, thin pieces. Mix it into the onions together with the tomatoes.

Watercress, apple and cheese salad

Finely chop the watercress. Core and chop the apple. Mix them together. Very thinly slice the onion and add it to taste. Beat together the oil, vinegar, salt and pepper and fold them into the salad. Mix in the cheese.

Fennel, cheese and walnut salad

Finely chop the fennel and mix it with the walnuts. Grate or crumble the cheese and cream it with a wooden spoon. Gradually beat in the yoghurt. Add the cayenne pepper and garlic. Mix in the fennel and walnuts.

Celery and cucumber with cheese topping

Put the cheese into a bowl and cream it. Mix in the parsley and garlic. Cut each celery stick into three pieces. Pile the cheese on top of the celery pieces and cucumber slices. Top each celery piece with an almond and the cucumber slices with a hazelnut.

Assembling the salads

Put equal portions of the salads onto each of 4 plates. Put a piece of celery in between them and a cucumber slice in the centre.

Nutty Salad Platter

Preparation time: 40 minutes
Waiting time: nil
Cooking time: nil

METRIC/IMPERIAL	AMERICAN

Mushroom, red pepper and sesame salad

METRIC/IMPERIAL	AMERICAN
100 g/4 oz button mushrooms	4 oz button mushrooms
1 red pepper	1 sweet red pepper
1½ tablespoons sesame seeds	1½ tablespoons sesame seeds
1 tablespoon chopped thyme	1 tablespoon chopped thyme
3 tablespoons sesame or sunflower oil	3 tablespoons sesame or sunflower oil
1½ tablespoons white wine vinegar	1½ tablespoons white wine vinegar
½ garlic clove, crushed with a pinch of sea salt	½ garlic clove, crushed with a pinch sea salt
pinch chilli powder	pinch chilli powder

Chickpea, peanut and raisin salad

METRIC/IMPERIAL	AMERICAN
75 g/3 oz cooked chickpeas	½ cup cooked chickpeas
40 g/1½ oz peanuts	¼ cup peanuts
40 g/1½ oz sultanas	¼ cup sultanas
2 tablespoons sunflower oil	2 tablespoons sunflower oil
1 tablespoon cider vinegar	1 tablespoon cider vinegar
¼ teaspoon curry powder	¼ teaspoon curry powder
1 tablespoon chopped fresh coriander or parsley	1 tablespoon chopped fresh coriander or parsley
1 garlic clove, crushed with a pinch sea salt	1 garlic clove, crushed with a pinch sea salt

Avocado salad

METRIC/IMPERIAL	AMERICAN
1 ripe avocado	1 ripe avocado
4 tablespoons natural yoghurt	¼ cup natural yoghurt
2 teaspoons tahini (sesame paste)	2 teaspoons tahini (sesame paste)
½ garlic clove, crushed with a pinch sea salt	½ garlic clove, crushed with a pinch sea salt
freshly ground black pepper	freshly ground black pepper
4 small parsley sprigs	4 small parsley sprigs

Hazelnut and tomato salad

4 tomatoes	4 tomatoes
50 g/2 oz watercress	2 oz watercress
75 g/3 oz hazelnuts	½ cup hazelnut meats
40 g/1½ oz raisins	¼ cup raisins
2 tablespoons sesame or sunflower oil	2 tablespoons sesame or sunflower oil
1 tablespoon white wine vinegar	1 tablespoon white wine vinegar
1 tablespoon chopped basil (or ½ tablespoon dried)	1 tablespoon chopped basil (or ½ tablespoon dried)
1 garlic clove, crushed with a pinch sea salt	1 garlic clove, crushed with pinch sea salt
pinch cayenne pepper	pinch cayenne pepper

Mushroom, red pepper and sesame salad

Thinly slice the mushrooms. Core and seed the pepper and cut it into 2.5 cm/1 inch strips. Mix the mushrooms and pepper with the sesame seeds and thyme. Beat together the oil, vinegar, garlic and chilli powder. Mix them into the rest.

Chickpea, peanut and raisin salad

Mix together the chickpeas, peanuts and sultanas. Beat together the oil, vinegar, curry powder, coriander and garlic. Fold them into the rest.

Avocado salad

Peel and dice the avocado. Beat togther the yoghurt, tahini, garlic and pepper. Mix in the avocado.

Hazelnut and tomato salad

Chop the tomatoes and watercress and mix them with the hazelnuts and raisins. Beat together the remaining ingredients and fold them into the salad.

Assembling the salads

Put a portion of the avocado salad in the centre of each of four plates. Top it with a parsley sprig. Arrange the other salads in portions around the edge.

Mixed Meat Platter

Preparation time: 40 minutes
Waiting time: nil
Cooking time: nil

METRIC/IMPERIAL	AMERICAN

Ham salad

METRIC/IMPERIAL	AMERICAN
175 g/6 oz cooked lean ham	6 oz cooked lean ham
1 dessert apple	1 dessert apple
225 g/8 oz Florence fennel or celery	½ lb Florence fennel or celery
2 tablespoons mayonnaise	2 tablespoons mayonnaise
1 tablespoon natural yoghurt	1 tablespoon natural yoghurt
½ teaspoon mustard powder	½ teaspoon mustard powder

Tongue salad

METRIC/IMPERIAL	AMERICAN
175 g/6 oz tongue	6 oz tongue
225 g/8 oz chicory	½ lb Belgian endive
1 large orange	1 large orange
25 g/1 oz currants	1 oz currants
2 tablespoons oil	2 tablespoons oil
1 tablespoon white wine vinegar	1 tablespoon white wine vinegar
1 teaspoon Dijon mustard	1 teaspoon Dijon mustard
½ garlic clove, crushed with pinch sea salt	½ garlic clove, crushed with pinch sea salt

Corned beef salad

METRIC/IMPERIAL	AMERICAN
175 g/6 oz corned beef	6 oz corned beef
100 g/4 oz watercress	¼ lb watercress
225 g/8 oz tomatoes	½ lb tomatoes
2 tablespoons oil	2 tablespoons oil
1 tablespoon white wine vinegar	1 tablespoon white wine vinegar
1 teaspoon tomato paste	1 teaspoon tomato paste
¼ teaspoon Tabasco sauce	¼ teaspoon Tabasco sauce
½ garlic clove, crushed with pinch sea salt	½ garlic clove, crushed with pinch sea salt
garnish:	*garnish:*
4 slices garlic sausage	4 slices garlic sausage
4 stuffed olives	4 stuffed olives
4 tomatoes	4 tomatoes

Ham salad

Chop the ham. Core and chop the apple. Chop the fennel. Put them into a bowl. Mix together the mayonnaise, yoghurt and mustard powder. Fold them into the ham.

Tongue salad

Chop the tongue. Thinly slice the chicory. Cut the rind and pith from the orange. Cut the flesh into lengthways quarters and thinly slice them. In a bowl, mix the tongue, chicory, orange and currants. Beat the oil, vinegar, mustard and garlic together and fold them into the salad.

Corned beef salad

Chop the corned beef, watercress and tomatoes and put them into a bowl. Beat the remaining ingredients together and fold them into the salad.

Assembling the salads

Put a slice of garlic sausage in the centre of each of four plates and top it with an olive. Put the salads round the edge, with a tomato wedge between each one.

RELISH TRAY

Grills and burgers are plain, no-nonsense foods and, if they are marinated or have tasty ingredients added, they should be able to stand up well on their own. However, no self-respecting fast food restaurant is without its tray of different coloured relishes and bowl of chopped raw onions. They are spooned not only over the meats but over potatoes and even the salad. You can also serve them with pizzas and pittas.

Bought relishes tend to be oversweetened and some may contain colourings or preservatives, so make your own. Not only will they be better for you, but they always taste better and you can add greater variety to the relish tray.

Unlike chutneys, relishes need only fairly small amounts of ingredients and a short cooking time, so you can prepare them just before a meal. They will not store indefinitely but will keep fresh in a covered plastic container in the refrigerator for up to a week.

Relishes are usually served cold, in separate bowls. However, for a change, you can make just one relish and serve it hot rather like a sauce.

Tomato, Celery & Red Pepper Relish

Preparation time: 10 minutes
Waiting time: 30 minutes
Cooking time: 15 minutes

METRIC/IMPERIAL	AMERICAN
225 g/8 oz tomatoes	½ lb tomatoes
2 large celery sticks	2 large celery sticks
1 red pepper	1 sweet red pepper
1 medium onion	1 medium onion
2 tablespoons olive oil	2 tablespoons olive oil
1 garlic clove, finely chopped	1 garlic clove, finely chopped
1 teaspoon celery seed	1 teaspoon celery seed
3 tablespoons white wine vinegar	3 tablespoons white wine vinegar

Scald, skin, seed and finely chop the tomatoes. Finely chop the celery. Core, seed and finely chop the pepper. Finely chop the onion.

Heat the oil in a saucepan on a low heat. Stir in the celery, onion, garlic and celery seed and cook them gently until the onion is transparent. Mix in the tomatoes and pepper.

Add the vinegar and let the mixture boil. Take the pan from the heat and transfer the relish to a bowl. Cool it completely before serving.

Serve with beef and lamb.

Sweet Pepper Relish

Preparation time: 5 minutes
Waiting time: 30 minutes
Cooking time: 15 minutes

METRIC/IMPERIAL	AMERICAN
1 green pepper	1 sweet green pepper
1 red pepper	1 sweet red pepper
1 large onion	1 large onion
3 tablespoons oil	3 tablespoons oil
1 tablespoon arrowroot	1 tablespoon arrowroot
4 tablespoons white wine vinegar	¼ cup white wine vinegar
1 teaspoon paprika	1 teaspoon paprika
¼ teaspoon Tabasco sauce	¼ teaspoon Tabasco sauce

Finely chop the peppers and the onion. Heat the oil in a saucepan on a low heat. Put in the peppers and onion and cook them until the onion begins to look transparent. Mix together the arrowroot, vinegar, paprika and Tabasco sauce. Add them to the pan and bring them to the boil. Cook, stirring, until the relish thickens, about 1½ minutes. Take the pan from the heat and turn the relish into a bowl to cool completely.

Serve with beef, pork and vegetarian burgers.

Mild Onion & Parsley Relish

Preparation time: 5 minutes
Waiting time: 30 minutes
Cooking time: 10 minutes

METRIC/IMPERIAL	AMERICAN
2 large onions	2 large onions
4 tablespoons oil	¼ cup oil
1 teaspoon ground cumin	1 teaspoon ground cumin
1 teaspoon ground coriander	1 teaspoon ground coriander
grated rind and juice ½ lemon	grated rind and juice ½ lemon
25 g/1 oz parsley, finely chopped	½ cup chopped parsley
150 ml/¼ pint natural yoghurt	⅝ cup natural yoghurt

Halve and thinly slice the onions. Heat the oil in a saucepan on a low heat. Stir in the onions, cumin and coriander and cook until the onions are transparent and just beginning to soften. Add the lemon rind and juice and let the juice boil.

Take the pan from the heat and stir in the parsley. Leave the onions to cool completely. Stir in the yoghurt.

Serve with lamb and bean dishes and beef dishes with a curry flavour.

Corn & Chilli Relish

Preparation time: 15 minutes
Waiting time: 30 minutes
Cooking time: 10 minutes

METRIC/IMPERIAL	AMERICAN
one 350 g/12 oz tin sweetcorn	one 12 oz can sweetcorn
1 tablespoon arrowroot	1 tablespoon arrowroot
2–4 red or green chillis, according to taste	2–4 red or green chillis, according to taste
1 yellow or green pepper	1 sweet yellow or green pepper
1 large onion	1 large onion
2 tablespoons oil	2 tablespoons oil

Drain the sweetcorn, reserving the liquid. Mix the liquid with the arrowroot. Core, seed and finely chop the chillis and the pepper. Finely chop the onion.

Heat the oil in a saucepan on a low heat. Put in the onion, pepper and chillis and cook until the onion begins to look transparent. Add the sweetcorn. Stir the liquid and arrowroot mixture and pour it into the pan. Stir until it thickens. Take the pan from the heat and turn the relish into a bowl to cool.

Sweet Onion & Lime Relish

Preparation time: 15 minutes
Waiting time: 30 minutes
Cooking time: 1 hour

METRIC/IMPERIAL	AMERICAN
3 large onions, halved and thinly sliced	3 large onions, halved and thinly sliced
grated rind and juice 2 limes	grated rind and juice 2 limes
2 tablespoons Barbados sugar	2 tablespoons Barbados sugar
½ teaspoon cayenne pepper	½ teaspoon cayenne pepper
2 tablespoons sunflower oil	2 tablespoons sunflower oil

Put all the ingredients into a saucepan. Cover them, set them on a high heat and bring them to the boil. Turn down the heat immediately and cook the relish gently for an hour stirring it from time to time. Cool.

The onions should be soft and brown and the mixture dry but not too sticky.

Serve with beef and lamb.

Lemon & Honey Relish

Preparation time: 10 minutes
Waiting time: 30 minutes
Cooking time: 1 hour

METRIC/IMPERIAL	AMERICAN
2 lemons	2 lemons
1 medium onion	1 medium onion
1 garlic clove	1 garlic clove
1 tablespoon honey	1 tablespoon honey
1 tablespoon olive oil	1 tablespoon olive oil
¼ teaspoon cayenne pepper	¼ teaspoon cayenne pepper

Cut the lemons into lengthways quarters and thinly slice them. Quarter and thinly slice the onion and finely chop the garlic. Put them all into a small saucepan with the rest of the ingredients and simmer them until you have a slightly sticky, light gold coloured relish. This will take about 1 hour.

Turn the relish into a bowl to cool.

Serve with lamb and pork.

Sweet & Sour Cucumber Relish

Preparation time: 15 minutes
Waiting time: 30 minutes
Cooking time: 5 minutes

METRIC/IMPERIAL	AMERICAN
1 cucumber	1 cucumber
1 medium onion	1 medium onion
2 teaspoons arrowroot	2 teaspoons arrowroot
1 teaspoon ground ginger	1 teaspoon ground ginger
150 ml/¼ pint white wine vinegar	⅝ cup white wine vinegar
1 tablespoon tamari, shoyu or soy sauce	1 tablespoon tamari, shoyu or soy sauce
2 tablespoons oil	2 tablespoons oil
2 teaspoons honey	2 teaspoons honey

Very finely chop the cucumber without peeling. Very finely chop the onion. Mix together the arrowroot, ginger, vinegar and soy sauce.

Heat the oil in a saucepan on a low heat. Put in the onion and cook until it becomes transparent, about 1½ minutes. Stir in the cucumber, arrowroot mixture and honey. Raise the heat and bring the mixture to the boil, stirring. Boil for about 2 minutes or until thickened. Take the pan from the heat and turn the relish into a bowl to cool completely.

Serve with beef, pork or lamb.

Plum Relish

Preparation time: 15 minutes
Waiting time: 30 minutes
Cooking time: 15 minutes

METRIC/IMPERIAL	AMERICAN
450 g/1 lb cooking plums	1 lb cooking plums
1 medium onion	1 medium onion
2 tablespoons oil	2 tablespoons oil
1 teaspoon mustard seed	1 teaspoon mustard seed
¼ teaspoon chilli powder	¼ teaspoon chilli powder
2 tablespoons red wine vinegar	2 tablespoons red wine vinegar
1 tablespoon molasses	1 tablespoon molasses

Finely chop the plums and the onion. Heat the oil in a saucepan on a low heat. Stir in the onion, mustard seed and chilli powder and cook, stirring occasionally, until the onion is soft.

Add the plums, vinegar and molasses and simmer, uncovered, for 15 minutes. Cool.

Serve with pork or lamb.

Apple & Date Relish

Preparation time: 15 minutes
Waiting time: 30 minutes
Cooking time: 30 minutes

METRIC/IMPERIAL	AMERICAN
450 g/1 lb cooking apples	1 lb cooking apples
50 g/2 oz stoned dates	2 oz stoned dates
1 small onion	1 small onion
4 tablespoons cider vinegar	¼ cup cider vinegar
pinch ground cloves	pinch ground cloves

Wipe, core and very finely chop the apples. Finely chop the dates and onion.

Put all the ingredients into a saucepan and set them on a low heat for 30 minutes, stirring occasionally. Cool.

Serve with pork and lamb.

Mustard Relish

Preparation time: 5 minutes
Waiting time: nil
Cooking time: 15 minutes

METRIC/IMPERIAL	AMERICAN
3 tablespoons oil	3 tablespoons oil
1 large onion, finely chopped	1 large onion, finely chopped
1 tablespoon wholewheat flour	1 tablespoon wholewheat flour
1 tablespoon mustard powder	1 tablespoon mustard powder
1 tablespoon ground turmeric	1 tablespoon ground turmeric
1 tablespoon ground ginger	1 tablespoon ground ginger
150 ml/¼ pint white wine vinegar	⅝ cup white wine vinegar

Heat the oil in a saucepan on a low heat. Mix in the onion and soften it. Stir in the flour, mustard, turmeric and ginger and stir for half a minute. Stir in the vinegar and stir until the mixture thickens.

This relish can be served hot or cold. As it cools, cover it with clingfilm or with dampened greaseproof paper to prevent a skin from forming on the top. Serve with beef and pork.

Horseradish & Orange Relish

Preparation time: 10 minutes
Waiting time: 30 minutes
Cooking time: nil

METRIC/IMPERIAL	AMERICAN
1 large orange	1 large orange
75 g/3 oz grated horseradish, preserved in vinegar	½ cup grated horseradish, preserved in vinegar
1 teaspoon mustard powder	1 teaspoon mustard powder
2 teaspoons white wine vinegar	2 teaspoons white wine vinegar
125 ml/4 fl oz soured cream	½ cup soured cream

Cut the rind and pith from the orange. Finely chop the flesh. Put the horseradish into a bowl and mix in the mustard powder, vinegar and soured cream. Mix in the pieces of orange. Leave the relish to stand for 30 minutes before serving. Serve with beef.

Uncooked Cranberry Relish

Preparation time: 15 minutes
Waiting time: 30 minutes
Cooking time: nil

METRIC/IMPERIAL	AMERICAN
225 g/8 oz cranberries	2 cups cranberries
grated rind and juice 1 large orange	grated rind and juice 1 large orange
2 tablespoons red wine vinegar	2 tablespoons red wine vinegar
2 tablespoons oil	2 tablespoons oil
1 medium onion, finely chopped	1 medium onion, finely chopped
¼ teaspoon ground allspice	¼ teaspoon ground allspice
50 g/2 oz dark Barbados sugar	¼ cup dark Barbados sugar

Put the cranberries and orange rind and juice into a liquidiser or food processor and work them to a rough purée.

Heat the oil in a frying pan on a low heat. Put in the onion and allspice and cook until the onion is soft. Stir in the sugar and stir until it melts.

Add the onion and sugar mixture to the cranberries and blend again. Chill for 30 minutes before serving.

Serve with turkey, chicken, lamb or pork.

Mushroom Relish

Preparation time: 10 minutes
Waiting time: 30 minutes
Cooking time: 10 minutes

METRIC/IMPERIAL	AMERICAN
225 g/8 oz open mushrooms	½ lb open mushrooms
3 tablespoons oil	3 tablespoons oil
1 medium onion, finely chopped	1 medium onion, finely chopped
1 garlic clove, finely chopped	1 garlic clove, finely chopped
4 tablespoons chopped parsley	¼ cup chopped parsley
1 tablespoon chopped thyme	1 tablespoon chopped thyme
½ teaspoon black peppercorns, coarsely crushed	½ teaspoon black peppercorns, coarsely crushed
4 tablespoons red wine vinegar	¼ cup red wine vinegar

Finely chop the mushrooms. Heat the oil in a saucepan on a low heat. Mix in the onions and garlic and cook them until the onion is transparent. Raise the heat to medium and add the mushrooms, herbs and peppercorns. Cook, stirring, until the mushrooms no longer look dry. Pour in the vinegar and bring it to the boil. Take the pan from the heat immediately and cool.

Serve with beef and lamb.

PIE STALL

Apple pies and turnovers are favourite sweets in fast food restaurants. They can be topped with whipped cream and eaten on the spot or taken away and eaten in the hand. At home, you don't have to stick to apples. Try cherries, blueberries or apricots and use dried fruit, fruit juice and other sweet fruit such as bananas for sweetening.

The traditional American pie pastry is light and crumbly and usually made with self raising flour and shortening. It can easily be made using a 100% wholewheat flour and bicarbonate of soda. Shortening, vegetable margerine or butter or a mixture of any two can be used. Instead of making turnovers with a puff or rough puff pastry, both of which are quite difficult to produce with a wholewheat flour, again add bicarbonate of soda for a light, crumbly effect. An ordinary, wholewheat shortcrust pastry could be used instead.

Another favourite fast food sweet is brownies. Brownies are usually made with chocolate or with cocoa powder but they are equally delicious if you use carob. Serve them warm with cream, or cold, topped with the yoghurt icing.

Double Crust Pie Pastry

Preparation time: 20 minutes
Waiting time: 30 minutes
Cooking time: 35 minutes

METRIC/IMPERIAL	AMERICAN
250 g/9 oz wholewheat flour	2¼ cups wholewheat flour
1 teaspoon bicarbonate of soda	1 teaspoon baking soda
pinch of fine sea salt	pinch fine sea salt
175 g/6 oz vegetable margarine or	1½ cups vegetable margarine or
shortening	shortening
3 tablespoons cold water	3 tablespoons cold water

Put the flour into a bowl with the bicarbonate of soda and salt. Rub in the margarine or shortening. Mix everything to a dough with the cold water. Leave the pastry in a cool place for 30 minutes.

Use two thirds of the pastry to line a 20 cm/8 inch diameter, 4 cm/1½ inch deep pie plate with sloping sides. Put in the filling. Cover it with the remaining pastry and seal the edges.

The pie should be baked for 35 minutes in a preheated 200C/400F/gas 6 oven.

Glazes for Double Crust Pie

A pie always looks much more attractive when it is glazed. Either brush it with beaten egg or milk before baking; or brush it with lightly beaten egg white, bake it for 25 minutes, brush it with egg white again and sprinkle it with 1 tablespoon Demerara sugar. Then return it to the oven for the final 10 minutes.

Turnover Pastry

Preparation time: 25 minutes
Waiting time: 30 minutes
Cooking time: 20 minutes

METRIC/IMPERIAL	AMERICAN
225 g/8 oz wholewheat flour	2 cups wholewheat flour
¼ teaspoon fine sea salt	¼ teaspoon fine sea salt
1 teaspoon bicarbonate of soda	1 teaspoon baking soda
50 g/2 oz vegetable margarine	½ cup vegetable margarine
50 g/2 oz shortening	½ cup shortening
4 tablespoons cold water	¼ cup cold water
filling:	*filling:*
1–2 tablespoons filling to each turnover	1–2 tablespoons filling to each turnover

Put the flour, salt and soda into a bowl. Rub in the margarine and shortening. Mix everything to a dough with cold water. Leave the pastry in a cool place for 30 minutes.

This amount will make 4 turnovers. Cut it into four pieces and roll each piece into a square or a circle.

Put 2 tablespoons of the filling on half of each piece. When using squares, this can be towards one side to make rectangular turnovers; or towards one corner to make triangles. The filling must not come closer than 1.5 cm/½ inch from the edge of the pastry.

Dampen the edges of the turnover with cold water. Fold half the pastry over the filling and press the edges together to seal them. Trim to neaten if necessary. Press the prongs of a fork all round the edges. Prick the tops of the turnovers several times with a fork to allow steam to escape.

Lift the turnovers onto a baking sheet and brush them with milk or with beaten egg. If wished, scatter them with chopped nuts or sesame or poppy seeds. Bake them for 20 minutes in a preheated 200C/400F/gas 6 oven.

Turnovers are best eaten hot or warm.

Easy Shortcrust Pastry

Preparation time: 10 minutes
Waiting time: nil
Cooking time: nil

METRIC/IMPERIAL	AMERICAN
225 g/8 oz wholewheat flour	2 cups wholewheat flour
pinch fine sea salt	pinch fine sea salt
100 g/4 oz vegetable margarine	1 cup vegetable margarine
4 tablespoons cold water	¼ cup cold water

Mix the flour and salt in a bowl and make a well in the centre. Put in the margarine and water. Stir with a fork until the mixture forms a dough.

Spiced Apple Pie

Preparation time: 20 minutes
Waiting time: nil
Cooking time: 35 minutes

METRIC/IMPERIAL	AMERICAN
double crust pastry made with	double crust pastry with
250 g/9 oz wholewheat flour	2¼ cups wholewheat flour
glaze as required	glaze as required
filling:	*filling:*
550 g/1 lb 4 oz cooking apples	1¼ cooking apples
1 teaspoon ground mixed spices	1 teaspoon ground mixed spices
50 g/2 oz sultanas	2 oz sultanas
50 g/2 oz light Barbados sugar	2 oz light Barbados sugar
4 tablespoons double cream	¼ cup heavy cream

Heat the oven to 200C/400F/gas 6. Peel, core and slice the apples and put them into a bowl. Mix in the spices, sultanas, sugar and cream.

Roll out two thirds of the pastry to line a 20 cm/8 inch diameter, 4 cm/1½ inch deep pie plate with sloping sides. Fill it with the apples. Cover them with the remaining pastry. Seal the edges and glaze as required (see basic method).

Bake the pie for 35 minutes or until golden brown. Serve it hot or warm with single (light) cream, soured cream or natural yoghurt.

Blueberry & Banana Pie

Preparation time: 30 minutes
Waiting time: nil
Cooking time: 35 minutes

METRIC/IMPERIAL	AMERICAN
double crust pastry made with	double crust pastry made with
250 g/9 oz wholewheat flour	2¼ cups wholewheat flour
glaze as required	glaze as required
filling:	*filling:*
450 g/1 lb blueberries	2½ cups blueberries
125 ml/4 fl oz red grape juice	½ cup red grape juice
1 tablespoon arrowroot	1 tablespoon arrowroot
1 large banana	1 large banana

Heat the oven to 200C/400F/gas 6. Put the blueberries into a saucepan with the grape juice. Cover them and set them on a low heat until they are soft and juicy, about 15 minutes.

Put the arrowroot into a bowl and mix in about 6 tablespoons/⅜ cup of the hot juice. Stir the mixture back into the blueberries. Put the saucepan back on the heat and bring the blueberries to the boil. Stir until the juice thickens, about 1½ minutes. Take the pan from the heat and leave the blueberries until they are cold.

Roll out two thirds of the pastry and line a 20 cm/8 inch diameter, 4 cm/1½ inch deep pie plate with sloping sides. Thinly slice the banana and cover the pastry base with the slices. Put in the blueberries. Cover them with the remaining pastry. Seal the edges and glaze as required (see basic method).

Bake the pie for 35 minutes or until golden brown. Serve it hot or warm with soured cream or natural yoghurt.

Honey & Lemon Meringue p. 129.
Pumpkin & Yoghurt Pie p. 126.
Spiced Apple Pie p. 123.

Opposite page 125:
Cherry Pie p. 125.
Blueberry & Banana Pie p. 124.
Raisin Brownies p. 134.

Cherry Pie

Preparation time: 25 minutes
Waiting time: 30 minutes
Cooking time: 35 minutes

METRIC/IMPERIAL	AMERICAN
double crust pastry made with	double crust pastry made with
250 g/9 oz wholewheat flour	2¼ cups wholewheat flour
1 egg white, lightly beaten	1 egg white lightly beaten
1 tablespoon Demerara	1 tablespoon Demerara sugar
filling:	*filling:*
550 g/1 lb 4 oz red cherries	1¼ lb red cherries
225 ml/8 fl oz red grape juice	1 cup red grape juice
2 tablespoons honey	2 tablespoons honey
2 tablespoons tapioca or sago	2 tablespoons tapioca or sago
¼ teaspoon almond essence	¼ teaspoon almond essence

Stone the cherries. Put them into a saucepan with the grape juice and honey. Set them on a medium heat and bring them to the boil. Take the pan from the heat. Stir in the tapioca or sago and almond essence. Leave the cherries to get completely cold.

Heat the oven to 200C/400F/gas 6. Roll out two thirds of the pastry and use it to line a 20 cm/8 inch diameter, 4 cm/1½ inches deep pie plate with sloping sides. Put in the cherry mixture. Cover it with the remaining pastry. Brush the pie with the beaten egg white and bake it for 25 minutes. Brush it again with the egg white and scatter with the demerara sugar. Return it to the oven for 10 minutes or until the top is golden.

Serve hot or warm.

Pumpkin & Yoghurt Pie

Serves 6
Preparation time: 30 minutes
Waiting time: 30 minutes
Cooking time: 1 hour 25 minutes

METRIC/IMPERIAL	AMERICAN
675 g/1½ lb slice pumpkin	1½ lb slice pumpkin
225 ml/8 fl oz natural yoghurt	1 cup natural yoghurt
4 eggs, beaten	4 eggs, beaten
100 g/4 oz Barbados or molasses sugar	½ cup Barbados or molasses sugar
1 teaspoon ground cinnamon	1 teaspoon ground cinnamon
¼ nutmeg grated	¼ nutmeg grated
turnover pastry made with	turnover pastry made with
175 g/6 oz wholewheat flour	1½ cups wholewheat flour

Heat the oven to 200C/400F/gas 6. Cut the rind and pith from the pumpkin. Chop the flesh into 2cm/¾ inch pieces. Wrap the pumpkin in lightly oiled foil and bake it for 40 minutes. Rub it through a sieve or mash it with a potato masher. Cool it.

Turn the oven to 180C/350F/gas 4. Beat the yoghurt into the eggs. Beat in the sugar and spices. Mix in the pumpkin. Roll out the pastry and line a 23 cm/9 inch diameter flan tin. Pour in the pumpkin mixture and bake the pie for 45 minutes or until the filling is set and browned.

Apricot Pie

Preparation time: 25 minutes
Waiting time: 30 minutes
Cooking time: 35 minutes

METRIC/IMPERIAL	AMERICAN
double crust pastry made with 250 g/9 oz wholewheat flour	double crust pastry made with 2¼ cups wholewheat flour
glaze as required	glaze as required
filling:	*filling:*
450 g/1 lb fresh apricots	1 lb fresh apricots
150 ml/¼ pint natural orange juice	⅝ cup natural orange juice
3 tablespoons honey	3 tablespoons honey
2 tablespoons tapioca or sago	2 tablespoon tapioca or sago

Halve and stone the apricots. Put them into a saucepan with the orange juice, honey and tapioca or sago. Set them on a low heat until the honey dissolves, and then bring them to the boil. Take the pan from the heat and leave the apricots until they are cold.

Roll out two thirds of the pastry and line a 20 cm/8 inch diameter 4 cm/1½ inch deep pie plate with sloping sides. Put in the filling. Cover it with the remaining pastry. Seal the edges and glaze as required.

Bake the pie for 35 minutes or until golden brown.

Honey & Molasses Pie

Preparation time: 15 minutes
Waiting time: nil
Cooking time: 25 minutes

METRIC/IMPERIAL	AMERICAN
shortcrust pastry made with	shortcrust pastry made with
225 g/8 oz wholewheat flour	2 cups wholewheat flour
50 g/2 oz desiccated coconut	¼ cup desiccated coconut
50 g/2 oz sugar-free meusli	⅓ cup sugar-free meusli
3 tablespoons honey	3 tablespoons honey
2 tablespoons molasses	2 tablespoons molasses
1 egg, beaten	1 egg, beaten

Heat the oven to 200C/400F/gas 6. Roll out two-thirds of the pastry and line a 20 cm/8 inch diameter flat pie plate. Roll out the remaining pastry and cut it into thin strips.

In a bowl, mix together the coconut, meusli, honey and molasses. Spread the mixture over the pastry. Make a lattice pattern on top with the pastry strips.

Brush the strips and the edges of the pie with beaten egg. Bake the pie for 25 minutes or until the pastry is golden brown.

Serve hot or cold.

Honey & Lemon Meringue

Preparation time: 30 minutes
Waiting time: 15 minutes
Cooking time: 45 minutes

METRIC/IMPERIAL	AMERICAN
pastry:	*pastry:*
225 g/8 oz wholewheat flour	2 cups wholewheat flour
pinch sea salt	pinch sea salt
175 g/6 oz butter, softened	¾ cup butter, softened
1 egg yolk	1 egg yolk
1 tablespoon honey	1 tablespoon honey
filling:	*filling:*
1½ tablespoons cornflour	1½ tablespoons cornflour
275 ml/1½ pint milk	1¼ cups milk
grated rind 1 lemon and juice of 1½	grated rind 1 lemon and juice of 1½
1 tablespoon honey	1 tablespoon honey
2 egg yolks	2 egg yolks
topping:	*topping:*
2 egg whites	2 egg whites
2 tablespoons honey	2 tablespoons honey

Heat the oven to 200C/400F/gas 6. Put the flour onto a work surface and scatter the salt over the top. Make a well in the centre and put in the butter, egg yolk and honey. Work the mixture to a smooth dough with your fingertips and set it aside for 15 minutes in a cool place. Roll it out and use it to line a 20 cm/8 inch flan tin. Bake the pastry blind for 15 minutes.

Mix the cornflour in a bowl with a little of the milk. Bring the rest of the milk to the boil in a saucepan and quickly stir it into the cornflour mixture. Pour the mixture back into the saucepan and bring it to the boil stirring, on a moderate heat.

Cook, stirring for about 3 minutes so you have a thick, smooth mixture.

Take the pan from the heat and beat in the honey, lemon rind and juice and egg yolks. Pour the mixture into the pastry base.

Turn the oven down to 170C/325F/gas 3 and bake the pie for 10 minutes.

Stiffly whip the egg whites and beat in the honey. Pile them on top of the lemon mixture and return the pie to the oven for 20 minutes or until the egg whites are golden brown.

Eat hot or warm.

Upside-Down Apple Cake

Preparation time: 30 minutes
Waiting time: 5 minutes
Cooking time: 20 minutes

METRIC/IMPERIAL	AMERICAN
100 g/4 oz butter, plus extra for greasing	½ cup butter, plus extra for greasing
150 g/5 oz clear honey	½ cup clear honey
100 g/4 oz wholewheat flour	1 cup wholewheat flour
½ teaspoon ground cinnamon	½ teaspoon ground cinnamon
freshly grated nutmeg, about ¼ nut	freshly grated nutmeg, about ¼ nut
1 teaspoon baking powder	1 teaspoon baking powder
2 eggs, beaten	2 eggs, beaten
1 large cooking apple	1 large cooking apple

Heat the oven to 180C/350F/gas 4. Beat the butter until it is soft and fluffy and beat in all but 2 tablespoons of the honey. Toss the flour, cinnamon, nutmeg and baking powder together. Beat the mixture into the butter, alternately with the eggs.

Butter an 18 cm/7 inch square cake tin. Peel, core and thinly slice the apple. Arrange the slices in the bottom of the tin and spoon over the remaining honey. Cover the apple with the cake mixture.

Bake the cake for 20 minutes or until the top is golden brown. Cool it in the tin for 5 minutes and turn it out, keeping it apple side up. Cut into squares and serve it hot or cold with whipped cream or natural yoghurt.

Apple & Strawberry Turnovers

Preparation time: 20 minutes
Waiting time: nil
Cooking time: 20 minutes

METRIC/IMPERIAL	AMERICAN
Turnover pastry made with	Turnover pastry made with
225 g/8 oz wholewheat flour	2 cups wholewheat flour
glaze as required	glaze as required
filling:	*filling:*
1 large cooking apple	1 large cooking appple
3 tablespoons sugar-free strawberry	3 tablespoons sugar-free strawberry
jam	jam

Heat the oven to 200C/400F/gas 6. Divide the pastry into four pieces and roll them out to the shape required. Peel, core and chop the apple and mix it with the jam.

Fill and shape the turnovers. Glaze them and bake as above.

Apple & Date Turnovers

Preparation time: 20 minutes
Waiting time: nil
Cooking time: 20 minutes

METRIC/IMPERIAL	AMERICAN
Turnover pastry made with	Turnover pastry made with
225 g/8 oz wholewheat flour	2 cups wholewheat flour
glaze as required	glaze as required
1 tablespoon sesame seeds	1 tablespoon sesame seeds
filling:	*filling:*
1 small cooking apple	1 small cooking apple
50 g/2 oz pressed dates	2 oz pressed dates
25 g/1 oz sunflower seeds	2 tablespoons sunflower seeds
1 tablespoon honey	1 tablespoon honey

Heat the oven to 200C/400F/gas 6. Divide the pastry into four pieces and roll them to the shape required. Peel, core and finely chop the apple. Finely chop the dates. Mix the apple and dates with the sunflower seeds and honey.

Fill and shape the turnovers. Glaze them and bake as above.

Dried Fruit & Lemon Turnovers

Preparation time: 20 minutes
Waiting time: 2 hours
Cooking time: 20 minutes

METRIC/IMPERIAL	AMERICAN
Turnover pastry made with	Turnover pastry made with
225 g/8 oz wholewheat flour	2 cups wholewheat flour
glaze as required	glaze as required
2 teaspoons poppy seeds	2 teaspoons poppy seeds
filling:	*filling:*
50 g/2 oz sultanas	⅓ cup sultanas
50 g/2 oz raisins	⅓ cup raisins
250 ml/8 fl oz natural orange juice	1 cup natural orange juice
25 g/1 oz shelled walnuts, finely chopped	1 oz chopped walnut meats
25 g/1 oz ground almonds	2 tablespoons ground almonds
2 teaspoons poppy seeds	2 teaspoons poppy seeds
½ teaspoon ground cinnamon	½ teaspoon ground cinnamon
grated rind 1 lemon	grated rind 1 lemon

Put the sultanas and raisins into a saucepan with the orange juice and bring them to the boil. Take the pan from the heat and leave them to soak for 2 hours. Drain them. Mix them with the walnuts, almonds, poppy seeds, cinnamon and lemon rind.

Heat the oven to 200C/400F/gas 6. Divide the pastry into four pieces and roll them to the shape required.

Fill and shape the turnovers. Glaze them and bake as above.

Carob Brownies

Serves 6-8
Preparation time: 25 minutes
Waiting time: 10 minutes
Cooking time: 25 minutes

METRIC/IMPERIAL	AMERICAN
75 g/3 oz vegetable margarine	⅜ cup vegetable margarine
75 g/3 oz Barbados sugar	¾ cup Barbados sugar
1 egg, beaten	1 egg, beaten
100 g/4 oz wholewheat flour	1 cup wholewheat flour
¼ teaspoon baking powder	¼ teaspoon baking powder
75 g/3 oz shelled walnuts, chopped	⅜ cup walnut meats
75 g/3 oz carob bar	3 oz carob bar
¼ teaspoon vanilla essence	¼ teaspoon vanilla essence
4 tablespoons milk	4 tablespons milk

Heat the oven to 180C/350F/gas 4. Cream the margarine with the sugar. Beat in the egg, a little at a time. Mix the flour with the baking powder and beat it into the mixture. Mix in the nuts.

Break up the carob bar and put it into a bowl. Stand the bowl in a saucepan of simmering water until the carob bar has melted. Beat the carob into the cake mixture with the vanilla essence and milk.

Put the mixture into a well greased 20 cm/8 inch square cake tin and bake it for 25 minutes or until firm. Cool the cake for 10 minutes in the tin. Turn it out and cut it into squares.

Serve the brownies warm, topped with natural yoghurt.

Raisin Brownies

Serves 8-10
Preparation time: 20 minutes
Waiting time: 30 minutes
Cooking time: 35 minutes, icing 10 minutes

METRIC/IMPERIAL	AMERICAN
450 g/1 lb wholewheat flour	4 cups wholewheat flour
50 g/2 oz carob powder	½ cup carob powder
250 g/8 oz vegetable margarine	1 cup vegetable margarine
175 g/6 oz dark Barbados sugar	1½ cups dark Barbados sugar
4 eggs, beaten	4 eggs, beaten
15 g/6 oz shelled walnuts, finely chopped	¾ cup chopped walnut meats
175 g/6 oz raisins	1 cup raisins
optional icing:	*optional icing:*
two 75 g/3 oz plain carob bars	two 3oz plain carob bars
½ pint natural yoghurt	1¼ cups natural yoghurt

Heat the oven to 160C/325F/gas 3. Mix together the flour and carob powder. Cream together the margarine and sugar. Beat in the flour, alternately with the eggs. Mix in the walnuts and raisins.

Put the mixture into a well greased 20 × 28 × 5 cm/8 × 11 × 2 inch tin and bake it for 35 minutes or until a skewer inserted into the centre comes out clean. Turn the cake onto a wire rack to cool completely.

To make the icing, break up the carob bars and put them into a bowl. Stand the bowl in a saucepan of water. Set it on a low heat for the carob to melt. Take the bowl from the pan and quickly beat in the yoghurt. Spread the icing over the cake.

To serve, cut the cake into small squares.

Note: This type of cake freezes well. Instead of icing the whole cake, half can be cut off and frozen and the other half spread with a half quantity of icing.

ICE-CREAM PARLOUR

Scoops of ice-cream, ice-cream made into sundaes, splits and knickerbocker glories — all are a pleasurable indulgence for adults and children alike. Piled high into tall glasses and topped with sauces, nuts, glacé fruits and cream, they are served in all fast food restaurants.

Bought ice-creams come in a wide variety of colours and flavours but their precise ingredients are generally unknown to the consumer. Are they dairy or non-dairy; and what exactly is 'non-dairy fat'? As long as you have a freezer or a refrigerator with a large, efficient freezing compartment, ice-creams will be easy to make at home from only natural ingredients.

Ice-creams can be made from cream alone; and for an end result that is still deliciously creamy but lower in fats and calories, use a mixture of double (heavy) cream and natural yoghurt. An ice made from yoghurt alone has a fresher flavour and provided it is beaten well during the freezing process, will still retain a creamy texture. Milk ice-creams are cheap and easy to make and the use of soya milk means that even those allergic to dairy products can enjoy ice-cream.

Flavour ice-creams with fresh or dried fruits, with spices such as vanilla or nutmeg, with essences such as peppermint and with carob powder or coffee. Sweeten when necessary with honey or raw sugar. When using soya milk, use flavourers that will complement or slightly mask its stronger taste.

Freezing Ice-Cream

Once the ice-cream mixture has been made, cool it completely if it is warm and then chill it for 1 hour in the refrigerator. If possible, put the mixture into a flat container. It will freeze more quickly in this than in a high sided bowl. If you are using the freezing compartment of the refrigerator, turn it to its lowest temperature whilst the mixture is chilling. In the freezer, leave space for air to circulate round the container. Freeze the mixture for three hours, stirring it every 30 minutes to make sure that it freezes evenly.

Turn the ice-cream into a bowl and beat it with an electric beater so that all the ice particles are broken up and you have a smooth slush. Put the ice-cream into a plastic container, cover it and freeze it for a further 2 hours. The ice-cream can be taken out and used immediately but it is best if left for a further few hours to mature.

If you intend to make ice-creams regularly, then it is worthwhile buying a small electric ice-cream machine that will fit inside the freezer and do all the stirring and beating for you. When the fan stops you know that you have the desirable semi-frozen, smooth slush. All you have to do then is put it into a container and freeze it for the final two hours.

After the final freezing, turn the refrigerator back to its normal setting. Depending on the star rating, ice-creams will keep for two weeks to 1 month in the freezing compartment of the refrigerator. In the freezer, they will keep for up to three months.

Serving Ice-Creams

Ideally, the ice-cream should be taken out of the freezer and be put into the refrigerator to soften before serving. 575–850 ml/1–1½ pints/2½–3¾ cups ice-cream will need to stay there for 45 minutes; 2.3 litres/4 pints/10 cups will need 4 hours. Sherbets thaw more quickly. 575–850 ml/1–1½ pints/2½–3¾ cups will only need 20 minutes in the refrigerator.

Ice-creams can be served with a tablespoon but a special scoop makes a more attractive presentation. Whichever you use, have them in a jug of hot water and dip them in it every time that you make a fresh scoop.

Sauces for ice-cream can be made from puréed soft fruits, either fresh, frozen or tinned in natural juices; or from dried fruits such as apricots that have been soaked in fruit juices and then liquidised. Chopped walnuts or pecan nuts, chopped toasted almonds or cashew nuts or toasted almond flakes all make an attractive decoration. Chopped candied or dried fruits can also be scattered over the top.

Vanilla Ice-Cream

Preparation time: 20 minutes
Waiting time: 6 hours
Cooking time: nil

METRIC/IMPERIAL	AMERICAN
2 egg yolks	2 egg yolks
50 g/2 oz honey	2 oz honey
½ pint double cream	1¼ cups heavy cream
1 vanilla pod or ½ teaspoon vanilla essence	1 vanilla pod or ½ teaspoon vanilla essence
½ pint natural yoghurt	1¼ cups natural yoghurt

Beat the egg yolks and honey in a bowl until they are light and fluffy. Put the cream and vanilla pod into a saucepan. Set them on a low heat and bring them gently to just below boiling point.

Take the pan from the heat and remove the vanilla pod. Beat the cream into the egg yolks and honey. Beat in the yoghurt. Freeze as above.

Note: If an all-cream ice-cream is required use 575 ml/1 pint/2½ cups double (heavy) cream and scald the whole amount with the vanilla pod.

Strawberry Ice-Cream

Preparation time: 20 minutes
Waiting time: 6 hours
Cooking time: nil

METRIC/IMPERIAL	AMERICAN
450 g/1 lb strawberries	1 lb strawberries
275 ml/½ pint double cream	1¼ cups heavy cream
4 tablespoons honey	4 tablespoons honey
275 ml/½ pint natural yoghurt	1¼ cups natural yoghurt

Chop the strawberries. Rub them through a sieve.

Lightly whip the cream and whip in the honey and then the yoghurt. Mix in the strawberry purée. Freeze as above.

Note: This ice-cream can be made with all double (heavy) cream instead of half yoghurt.

Butterscotch Pecan Ice-Cream

Preparation time: 25 minutes
Waiting time: 6 hours
Cooking time: nil

METRIC/IMPERIAL	AMERICAN
275 ml/½ pint double cream	1¼ cups heavy cream
1 vanilla pod or ¼ teaspoon vanilla essence	1 vanilla pod or ¼ teaspoon vanilla essence
2 egg yolks	2 egg yolks
50 g/2 oz dark Barbados sugar	½ cup dark Barbados sugar
6 tablespoons water	⅜ cup water
275 ml/½ pint natural yoghurt	1¼ cups natural yoghurt
75 g/3 oz shelled pecan nuts, chopped	¾ cup chopped pecan nut meats

Put the cream into a saucepan with the vanilla pod or essence and set it on a very low heat. Bring it to simmering point. Take the pan from the heat and remove the vanilla pod.

Beat the egg yolks until they are light coloured and frothy. Put the sugar and water into a saucepan. Set them on a low heat and stir for the sugar to dissolve. Boil the syrup for 10 minutes and then immediately dip the base of the pan into cold water to stop the cooking process.

Whisk the syrup into the egg yolks. Continue whisking until the mixture is thick. Whisk in the cream and then the yoghurt. Mix in the nuts.

Freeze as above.

Note: Walnuts may be used if pecan nuts are not available. If an all-cream ice-cream is required, use 575 ml/1 pint/2½ cups double (heavy) cream and scald the whole amount with the vanilla pod.

Pina Colada Ice-Cream

Preparation time: 15 minutes
Waiting time: 6 hours
Cooking time: nil

METRIC/IMPERIAL	AMERICAN
1 medium pineapple	1 medium pineapple
275 ml/½ pint double cream	1¼ cups heavy cream
4 tablespoons honey	4 tablespoons honey
275 ml/½ pint natural yoghurt	1¼ cups natural yoghurt
50 g/2 oz candied peel, very finely chopped	2 oz candied peel, very finely chopped

Cut the husk from the pineapple. Cut the flesh into slices. Core and chop them. Put the chopped pineapple into a blender or food processor and liquidise it.

Lightly whip the cream and whip in the honey and then the yoghurt. Mix in the pineapple and the candied peel. Freeze as above.

Note: This ice-cream can be made using all double (heavy) cream instead of half yoghurt.

Banana Yoghurt Ice

Preparation time: 20 minutes
Waiting time: 6 hours
Cooking time: nil

METRIC/IMPERIAL	AMERICAN
4 ripe bananas	4 ripe bananas
juice ½ lime or lemon	juice ½ lime or lemon
freshly grated nutmeg	freshly grated nutmeg
2 egg yolks	2 egg yolks
50 g/2 oz honey	2 oz honey
575 ml/1 pint natural yoghurt	2½ cups natural yoghurt

Mash and sieve the bananas. In a large bowl mix them with the lemon juice and about one eighth of a nutmeg.

Beat the egg yolks until they are light and fluffy. Bring the honey to just below boiling point. Beat it into the egg yolks and beat the mixture to a foam. Beat the yolks and honey into the bananas. Mix in the yoghurt. Freeze as above.

Vanilla Yoghurt Ice

Preparation time: 20 minutes
Waiting time: 6 hours
Cooking time: nil

METRIC/IMPERIAL	AMERICAN
2 egg yolks	2 egg yolks
50 g/2 oz honey	2 oz honey
575 ml/1 pint natural yoghurt	2½ cups natural yoghurt
½ teaspoon vanilla essence	½ teaspoon vanilla essence

Beat the egg yolks until they are light and fluffy. Bring the honey to just below boiling point. Beat it into the egg yolks and beat in the mixture to a foam.

Beat in the yoghurt and the vanilla essence.

Freeze as above.

Ambrosia Yoghurt Ice

Preparation time: 40 minutes
Waiting time: 6 hours
Cooking time: nil

METRIC/IMPERIAL	AMERICAN
½ medium sized fresh coconut	½ medium sized fresh coconut
grated rind and juice of 1 large orange	grated rind and juice of large orange
2 egg yolks	2 egg yolks
50 g/2 oz honey	50 g/2 oz honey
575 ml/1 pint natural yoghurt	2½ cups natural yoghurt

Finely grate the coconut and mix it with the orange rind and juice.

Beat the egg yolks until they are light abd fluffy. Bring the honey to just below boiling point. Beat it into the egg yolks and beat the mixture to a foam.

Mix in the coconut and beat in the yoghurt.

Freeze as above.

Carob Milk Ice-Cream

Preparation time: 20 minutes
Waiting time: 6 hours
Cooking time: nil

METRIC/IMPERIAL	AMERICAN
25 g/1 oz carob powder	1 oz carob powder
25 g/1 oz arrowroot	1 oz arrowroot
850 ml/1½ pints milk or soya milk	4¾ cups milk or soya milk
100 g/4 oz honey	⅓ cup honey

In a bowl, mix together the carob powder and arrowroot. Mix in 150 ml/¼ pint of the milk so you have a thin, smooth paste. Put the remaining milk into a saucepan and stir in the honey. Stir on a low heat until the honey has dissolved. Bring the milk to just below boiling point. Stir it into the carob mixture. Return the mixture to the saucepan and bring it to the boil, stirring. Boil for about 2 minutes for the mixture to thicken. Cool it, chill it and then freeze it as above.

Carob and Raisin Ice-Cream

Make as above, adding 100 g/4 oz raisins when the mixture is returned to the saucepan.

Carob, Rum and Raisin Ice-Cream

Soak the raisins in 6 tablespoons rum for at least 4 hours. Drain them. Add them to the mixture after it has been chilled.

Opposite page 140:
Clockwise from top left:
Ambrosia Yoghurt Ice p. 140.
Carob Milk Ice-Cream p. 141.
Cranberry & Yoghurt Sherbet p. 143.
Pina Colada Ice-Cream p. 139.
Apricot & Yoghurt Sherbert p. 142.

Top: Fruit Sunrise p. 150
Orange, Lemon & Banana Shake p. 151.
Grapefruit, Pineapple & Banana Crush p. 151.
Bottom: Pink Fizz p. 154
Blackcurrant Yoghurt Fizz p. 153.

Maple Syrup & Peanut Milk Ice

Preparation time: 25 minutes
Waiting time: 6 hours
Cooking time: nil

METRIC/IMPERIAL	AMERICAN
25 g/1 oz arrowroot	1 oz arrowroot
850 ml/1½ pints milk or soya milk	4¾ cups soya milk
150 g/5 oz peanuts	1 cup peanuts
100 g/4 oz maple syrup	⅓ cup maple syrup

Put the arrowroot into a bowl. Mix in 150 ml/¼ pint/⅝ cup of the milk so you have a thin, smooth paste. Bring the remaining milk to just below boiling point. Take it off the heat. Stir in the arrowroot mixture. Set the saucepan back on the heat and bring the mixture to the boil, stirring. Boil for about 2 minutes for the mixture to thicken. Remove from the heat.

Finely chop or grind the peanuts. Put the maple syrup into a saucepan and bring it to just below boiling point, stir in the peanuts and cook them for 1 minute, stirring. Take the pan from the heat and stir in the milk.

Chill and freeze as above.

Apricot & Yoghurt Sherbet

Preparation time: 20 minutes
Waiting time: 8 hours
Cooking time: 20 minutes

METRIC/IMPERIAL	AMERICAN
175 g/6 oz dried whole apricots	6 oz dried whole apricots
275 ml/½ pint natural orange juice	1¼ cups natural orange juice
2 tablespoons honey	2 tablespoons honey
275 ml/½ pint water	1¼ cups water
150 ml/¼ pint natural yoghurt	⅝ cup natural yoghurt

Soak the apricots in the orange juice for 2 hours. Put them into a saucepan, bring them gently to the boil and simmer them for 20 minutes or until they are plump and tender. Add the honey. Liquidise the apricots, juice and honey. Add the water and liquidise again. Chill.

If you are using an ice-cream machine, add the yoghurt now. Put it into a bowl and beat in the thinned apricot purée. Freeze according to instructions. If you are freezing and beating the mixture, freeze it to a slush as for ice-cream. Whip it, whip in the yoghurt and freeze completely.

Cranberry & Yoghurt Sherbet

Preparation time: 25 minutes
Waiting time: 6 hours
Cooking time: 15 minutes

METRIC/IMPERIAL	AMERICAN
225 g/8 oz cranberries	2 cups cranberries
275 ml/½ pint red grape juice	1¼ cups red grape juice
175 g/6 oz honey	½ cup honey
275 ml/½ pint water	1¼ cups water
150 ml/¼ pint natural yoghurt	⅝ cup natural yoghurt

Put the cranberries into a bowl with the grape juice. Cover them and set them on a low heat for 15 minutes or until they are soft and juicy. Rub them through a sieve.

Return the purée to the cleaned saucepan. Add the honey and stir on a low heat for it to dissolve. Add the water and bring to the boil. Take the pan from the heat and chill the mixture.

If you are using an ice-cream machine add the yoghurt now. Put it into a bowl and beat in the cranberry purée. Freeze according to instructions. If you are freezing and beating the mixture, freeze it to a slush as for ice-cream. Whip it, whip in the yoghurt and freeze completely.

Sauces

Strawberry Sauce

Rub 225 g/8 oz/½ lb strawberries through a sieve. Put them into a saucepan and add 2 tablespoons honey. Stir on a low heat for the honey to dissolve.

Turn the sauce into a bowl. Cool it and chill it for about 1½ hours.

Raspberry Sauce

Put 350 g/12 oz/¾ lb fresh or frozen raspberries with 4 tablespoons honey into a saucepan. Set them on a low heat for 10 minutes or until the raspberries are soft and juicy.

Rub the raspberries through a sieve. Cool and chill the purée for about 1½ hours.

Blackcurrant Sauce

Put the blackcurrants and the juice from a 225 g/8 oz/½ lb tin of blackcurrants through a sieve. Stir to mix well and chill for about 1 hour.

Apricot Sauce

Soak 100 g/4 oz/¼ lb dried apricots in 150 ml/¼ pint/⅝ cup natural orange or pineapple juice for 8 hours. Liquidise them with the juice and chill the resulting purée for about 1 hour.

Carob Sauce

Put 75 g/3 oz/⅜ cup Barbados sugar and 125 g/4 fl oz/½ cup water into a saucepan. Set them on a low heat and stir until the sugar has dissolved. Raise the heat and boil the syrup for 5 minutes.

Break up a 75 g/3 oz plain carob bar. Put the pieces either into a double boiler or into a bowl standing in a saucepan of water. Melt it gently on a low heat.

Take the melted carob off the heat and gradually stir in the syrup. Beat until the sauce is glossy. Serve it hot or cold.

SUNDAES AND SPLITS

You can make these special ice-cream treats as large or as small as you like. You do not have to pile six scoops into a huge tall glass. You can make something a little more easy to eat by simply using two or three scoops togther with different sauces and garnishes and perhaps a topping of whipped cream or a thick natural yoghurt.

Carob Sundae

Serves 1
Preparation time: 10 minutes

METRIC/IMPERIAL	AMERICAN
2 tablespoons carob sauce	2 tablespoons carob sauce
4 teaspoons chopped walnuts	4 teaspoons chopped walnut meats
2 scoops carob ice-cream	2 scoops carob ice-cream
1 or 2 scoops vanilla or Ambrosia ice-cream	1 or 2 scoops vanilla or Ambrosia ice-cream
1 tablespoon chopped raisins	1 tablespoon chopped raisins
1 tablespoon whipped cream or thick natural yoghurt	1 tablespoon whipped cream or thick natural yoghurt
1 walnut half	1 walnut half

Pour 1 tablespoon of the carob sauce round the edges of a tall glass or glass dish. Put in half the chopped walnuts to stick to the sides of the glass. Put in the scoops of ice-cream and pour the remaining sauce over them.

Scatter in the raisins. Top with the whipped cream or yoghurt and the walnut half.

Strawberry Sundae

Serves 1
Preparation time: 10 minutes

METRIC/IMPERIAL	AMERICAN
2 tablespoons strawberry sauce	2 tablespoons strawberry sauce
2 scoops strawberry ice-cream	2 scoops strawberry ice-cream
1 or 2 scoops vanilla or banana ice-cream	1 or 2 scoops vanilla or banana ice-cream
3 fresh strawberries	3 fresh strawberries
1 tablespoon whipped cream or thick natural yoghurt	1 tablespoon whipped cream or thick natural yoghurt
1 teaspoon chopped toasted hazelnuts	1 teaspoon chopped toasted hazelnuts

Pour 1 tablespoon of the strawberry sauce round the edges of a tall glass or a glass dish. Put in the scoops of ice-cream and then spoon in the remaining sauce. Chop two of the strawberries and scatter them over the top.

Put on the cream or yoghurt. Scatter it with the hazelnuts and top with a whole strawberry.

Banana Split

Serves 1
Preparation time: 10 minutes

METRIC/IMPERIAL	AMERICAN
1 banana	1 banana
1 scoop vanilla ice-cream	1 scoop vanilla ice-cream
1 scoop Ambrosia ice-cream	1 scoop Ambrosia ice-cream
1 scoop Pina Colada ice-cream	1 scoop Pina Colada ice-cream
2 tablespoons apricot sauce	2 tablespoons apricot sauce
2 tablespoons raspberry or strawberry sauce	2 tablespoons raspberry or strawberry sauce
1 tablespoon toasted almond flakes	1 tablespoon toasted almond flakes
3 whole almonds	3 whole almonds

Cut the banana in half lengthways. Put the halves, one each side of a long dish, the curves going outwards. Put the three scoops of ice-cream between them.

Spoon the apricot sauce over the ice-creams and the raspberry sauce over the banana. Scatter the almond flakes over the banana and top each scoop of ice-cream with a whole almond.

Note: If all varieties of ice-cream are not available use two or even one.

ICED LOLLIES

Iced lollies are easy to make from fruit juices, or from yoghurt or milk mixtures. Chill the mixture for at least thirty minutes before pouring it into plastic lolly moulds and freezing until hard. There is no need for stirring or beating since a soft melting texture is not required.

Orange & Lemon Lollies

Preparation time: 10 minutes
Waiting time: 3½ hours
Cooking time: nil

METRIC/IMPERIAL	AMERICAN
1 lemon	1 lemon
1 tablespoon honey	1 tablespoon honey
575 ml/1 pint natural orange juice	1 pint natural orange juice

Grate the lemon rind into a jug or bowl. Cut the pith from the lemon. Thinly slice the flesh and add it to the rind. Put in the honey.

Bring the orange juice to just below boiling point. Pour it over the lemon and leave it until it is cold.

Pour off the juice, but do not sieve it so that the lemon rind is kept. Freeze as above.

Apple & Yoghurt Lollies

Preparation time: 15 minutes
Waiting time: 2 hours
Cooking time: 20 minutes

METRIC/IMPERIAL	AMERICAN
2 dessert apples	2 dessert apples
275 ml/½ pint natural yoghurt	½ pint natural yoghurt
2 tablespoons concentrated apple juice	2 tablespoons concentrated apple juice

Heat the oven to 200C/400F/gas 6. Core the apples. Put them into a heatproof dish and pour in about 6 mm/¼ inch water. Bake them for 20 minutes or until they are soft. Skin them and rub them through a sieve.

Mix the concentrated juice into the apples and gradually beat in the yoghurt.

Freeze as above.

DRINKS BAR

Whether it be a colourful cocktail or a rich, creamy milk shake, the drink served with a fast food meal should be just as important as the food. Water, preferably mineral water, topped up with crushed ice should always be on the table. A fruit juice cocktail makes a perfect starter; and a milk or yoghurt drink can be served in place of (or even with!) the sweet.

Fruit cocktails can be made from freshly squeezed or carton packed fruit juices or a mixture. Serve them undiluted or half and half with a sparkling mineral water to make them really refreshing and thirst quenching. You can use all the same garnishes on all juice cocktails as you can with alcoholic ones. Cut fresh fruits into attractive slices and skewer them on decorated cocktail sticks with maraschino or stoned fresh cherries. Serve cocktails and juices in tall, slim glasses or conical cocktail glasses. Balance the skewered fruits across the top and put in a coloured plastic straw.

If you mix sparkling mineral water with fruit juice and whizz them in a liquidiser with some ice-cream, you have an ice-cream soda. Mineral water also mixes surprisingly well with milk, or yoghurt to make a drink with a richer flavour.

Milk alone makes the most creamy milk shake, especially when topped up with an ice-cream containing double (heavy) cream. For a more refreshing flavour mix milk with an equal quantity of natural yoghurt.

Soya milk can be used for non-dairy shakes and sodas, either alone or mixed with mineral water. Flavour it with fruit sauces, puréed banana or soya milk ice-cream.

Citrus Cocktail

Serves 2
Preparation time: 10 minutes

METRIC/IMPERIAL	AMERICAN
juice ½ grapefruit	juice ½ grapefruit
juice ½ lemon	juice ½ lemon
juice ½ orange	juice ½ orange
275 ml/½ pint pineapple juice	1¼ cups pineapple juice
½ slice pineapple	½ slice pineapple
4 maraschino or fresh cherries	4 maraschino or fresh cherries

Put the fresh juices and pineapple juice into a liquidiser and blend them well. Divide the cocktail between two glasses.

Cut the piece of pineapple into two fan-shaped pieces and secure each one on a cocktail stick between two cherries.

Lay a stick over the top of each glass.

Fruit Sunrise

Serves 1
Preparation time: 10 minutes

METRIC/IMPERIAL	AMERICAN
100 ml/3½ fl oz natural orange juice	⅜ cup natural orange juice
100ml/3½ fl oz natural grapefruit juice	⅜ cup natural grapefruit juice
4 ice cubes	4 ice cubes
1 teaspoon syrop de grendine (non-alcoholic)	1 teaspoon syrop de grendine (non-alcoholic)
1 slice orange	1 slice orange
1 slice grapefruit	1 slice grapefruit
2 maraschino cherries	2 maraschino cherries

Mix together the orange and grapefruit juice. Put the ice into a conical shaped glass and pour in the mixed juices. Dash the syrop round the sides of the glass and wait until it sinks to the bottom before serving.

Make the orange and grapefruit slices into twists. Secure them on a cocktail stick with the cherries between. Lay the stick across the top of the glass.

Orange, Lemon & Banana Shake

Preparation time: 10 minutes

METRIC/IMPERIAL	AMERICAN
1 litre/1 pint 12 oz natural orange juice	4 cups natural orange juice
juice 1 lemon	juice 1 lemon
2 bananas, sliced	2 bananas, sliced
1 banana cut into four	1 banana cut into four
8 maraschino cherries	8 maraschino or fresh cherries

Put the orange juice, lemon juice and sliced bananas into a liquidiser and blend them well. Pour into 4 glasses.

Put a piece of the remaining banana onto each of four cocktail sticks with a cherry on either end. Lay the sticks across the tops of the glasses.

Grapefruit, Pineapple & Banana Crush

Preparation time: 10 minutes

METRIC/IMPERIAL	AMERICAN
500 ml/16 fl oz natural grapefruit juice	2 cups natural grapefruit juice
500 ml/16 fl oz pineapple juice	2 cups pineapple juice
2 bananas sliced	2 bananas, sliced
225 g/8 oz fresh pineapple, diced (or pineapple tinned in natural juice)	½ lb fresh pineapple, diced (or pineapple tinned in natural juice)
1 slice pineapple, cut into quarters	1 slice pineapple, cut into quarters
4 orange slices	4 orange slices
4 maraschino or fresh cherries	4 maraschino or fresh cherries

Put the grapefruit juice, pineapple juice, bananas and diced pineapple into a liquidiser and blend well. Pour into four glasses.

Put a piece of pineapple, a twisted orange slice and a cherry onto each of four cocktail sticks. Lay a stick across the top of each glass.

Coconut Cocktail

Preparation time: 5 minutes

METRIC/IMPERIAL
225 ml/8 fl oz coconut milk
225 ml/8 fl oz natural orange juice
225 ml/8 fl oz natural pineapple juice

AMERICAN
1 cup coconut milk
1 cup natural orange juice
1 cup natural pineapple juice

Put all the ingredients into a liquidiser and work them until they are well mixed and frothy.

As an optional garnish thread two halves of an orange slice, two halves of a pineapple slice and one glacé cherry onto a cocktail stick. Balance it over the top of the glass.

Pineapple Ice-Cream Soda

Serves 1
Preparation time: 5 minutes

METRIC/IMPERIAL
125 ml/4 fl oz pineapple juice
125 ml/4 fl oz sparkling mineral water
2 tablespoons vanilla ice-cream or
yoghurt ice

AMERICAN
½ cup pineapple juice
½ cup sparkling mineral water
2 tablespoons vanilla ice-cream or
yoghurt ice

Put the pineapple juice, mineral water and half the ice-cream into a liquidiser. Work them to a pale, frothy liquid.

Pour the drink into a glass and top it with the remaining ice-cream.

Strawberry Milk Soda

Serves 1
Preparation time: 5 minutes

METRIC/IMPERIAL	AMERICAN
125 ml/4 fl oz milk	½ cup milk
125 ml/4 fl oz sparkling mineral water	½ cup sparkling mineral water
2 tablespoons strawberry sauce (page 144)	2 tablespoons strawberry sauce (page 144)
2 tablespoons strawberry ice-cream	2 tablespoons strawberry ice-cream

Put the milk, mineral water, strawberry sauce and half the ice-cream into a liquidiser. Work them to a frothy liquid.

Pour the drink into a glass and top it with the remaining ice-cream.

Blackcurrant Yoghurt Fizz

Serves 1
Preparation time: 5 minutes

METRIC/IMPERIAL	AMERICAN
2 tablespoons blackcurrant sauce (page 144)	2 tablespoons blackcurrant sauce (page 144)
150 ml/¼ pint sparkling mineral water	⅝ cup sparkling mineral water
90 ml/3 fl oz natural yoghurt	⅜ cup natural yoghurt
2 tablespoons yoghurt vanilla ice-cream	2 tablespoons yoghurt vanilla ice-cream

Put the blackcurrant purée, mineral water, yoghurt and half the ice-cream into a liquidiser and work them to a frothy liquid.

Pour the drink into a glass and top it with the remaining ice-cream.

Pink Fizz

Serves 2
Preparation time: 10 minutes

METRIC/IMPERIAL	AMERICAN
100 ml/3½ fl oz natural grapefruit juice	⅜ cup natural grapefruit juice
100 ml/3½ fl oz natural pineapple juice	⅜ cup natural pineapple juice
2 teaspoons grenadine	2 teaspoons grenadine
4 ice cubes	4 ice cubes
200 ml/7 fl oz sparkling mineral water	⅞ cup sparkling mineral water
2 slices lemon	2 slices lemon
4 maraschino cherries	4 maraschino cherries

Shake the fruit juices, grenadine and ice cubes in a cocktail shaker. Divide them between two tall glasses and top them up with the mineral water.

Make the lemon slices into twists and skewer each one on a cocktail stick between two cherries.

Strawberry Yoghurt Shake

Preparation time: 5 minutes

METRIC/IMPERIAL	AMERICAN
125 ml/4 fl oz milk	½ cup milk
125 ml/4 fl oz natural yoghurt	½ cup natural yoghurt
4 tablespoons strawberry sauce (page 144)	¼ cup strawberry sauce (page 144)
1 tablespoon strawberry or vanilla ice-cream or yoghurt ice	1 tablespoon strawberry or vanilla ice-cream or yoghurt ice

Put the milk, yoghurt and strawberry sauce into a liquidiser and work them until they are frothy.

Pour the shake into a tall glass and top it with the ice-cream.

Raspberry Yoghurt Shake

Make as for strawberry, only using 6 tablespoons/⅜ cup raspberry sauce (page 144) instead of the strawberry vanilla yoghurt ice.

Carob Milk Shake I

Serves 1
Preparation time: 10 minutes
Waiting time: 30 minutes

METRIC/IMPERIAL	AMERICAN
1½ teaspoon carob powder	1½ teaspoons carob powder
250 ml/8 fl oz milk	1 cup milk
1 teaspoon honey	1 teaspoon honey
2 tablespoons vanilla ice-cream	2 tablespoons vanilla ice-cream
1 cube carob bar	1 cube carob bar

Put the carob powder into bowl and mix in 3 tablespoons of the milk to make a smooth paste. Bring the remaining milk to the boil and stir it into the paste. Leave the mixture to cool completely and then chill it for 30 minutes.

Put the mixture into a liquidiser with the honey and 1 tablespoon of the ice-cream. Work it until it is frothy. Pour the shake into a tall glass.

Top it with the remaining ice-cream and grate in the piece of carob bar.

Carob Milk Shake II

Serves 1
Preparation time: 5 minutes

METRIC/IMPERIAL	AMERICAN
250 ml/8 fl oz milk or soya milk	1 cup milk or soya milk
3 tablespoons carob milk ice-cream	3 tablespoons carob milk ice-cream
1 cube carob bar	1 cube carob bar

Put the milk into a liquidiser with 2 tablespoons of the ice-cream. Work it until it is frothy.

Pour the shake into a tall glass. Float the remaining ice-cream on top and grate in the cube of carob bar.